SEEKING

AN ENCOUNTER WITH SPIRITUAL ECSTASY AND ITS AFTERMATH

A Memoir

by

Paul Moser

Currach Press

Published in the United States and the United Kingdom by Currach Press

ISBN 978-0-9847941-6-4 (pbk.)
ISBN 978-0-9847941-7-1 (ebk.)

First edition 2019

Printed in the United States of America

1 2 3 4 5 6 7 8 9 10

A NOTE ON DIALOGUE AND PSEUDONYMS

This is a true story. That being said, it is reasonable to ask how I, with a legendarily rotten memory, could possibly have remembered so much precise dialogue among so many characters, over so many intervening years. The answer is: I couldn't. It is true, however, that the most pivotal scenes in the story contain thoughts and speech that are recorded virtually word-for-word, as a result of being burned into my consciousness. It is also true that I re-created much dialogue based on what I remember of the mood and outcome of each particular scene.

Most of the names in the story have been changed to protect all of us from lawyers. The most notable exceptions to this rule are my great friends, Alan and Helen Hooker, who, though no longer in their bodies, are very much alive in my heart, and whom I firmly believe would have no objection to being identified.

"After the ecstasy, the laundry."
–Jack Kornfield

For Alan and Helen

INTRODUCTION

Like so many love stories, this one is full of irrational behavior, regrettable scenes, and flat-out craziness. Unlike most love stories, it does not include a conventional pair of lovers, but instead concerns a zealous individual and his search for love and meaning through arduous, lone-wolf spiritual practices.

It's the story of someone with a particular form of the Seeking Syndrome, a condition that affects everyone to a greater or lesser degree, manifesting as a restlessness that pushes us, sometimes recklessly, toward a liberating something, an expansiveness, a hard-to-define sense of fulfillment just beyond our ken. Examples are not hard to find: from an elaborate assault on K-2 to an expensive sweat-lodge weekend in Sedona, from NASA space shots to tequila shots at the corner bar, there is plenty of evidence that the raw itch for transcendence is going to get scratched one way or another.

It was this itch that drew an earnest young person into the sphere of metaphysics and meditation, harnessing fervent, ungovernable desire to tenacious self-examination. Metaphorically—and only half-jokingly—you could say it is what happens when you give a powerful magnifying glass and a good pair of tweezers to someone who is already obsessed with lint.

It is inevitable that the events recounted here be interpreted by some as a cautionary tale about the dangers of introspection, and rightly so. We all have heard this one in some form or another. You know: Rather than sit in a tree and contemplate your navel, you should be *out there*, engaged in the world, making your way, doing well by doing good. How can it serve any good purpose to risk getting lost in one's own mind?

I very much empathize with this point of view. When you look at the terrible mess that our world appears to be, you don't have to be Mother Teresa to realize it can use some help. Your help. Your money, your kindness, your elbow grease at the charity spaghetti feed or the soup kitchen. With all the hot-button emergencies around us, it is reasonable to object to the notion of sitting very still in a room for hours at a time, or even to the very notion of self-exploration. The whole thing smells of self-indulgence. But, to suggest a broader view of what might be helpful to our world and our lives in it, I would offer a couple of additional points.

First: The world is wide, and help can take many forms, some more visible than others. And there must have been a reason that no less a figure than Socrates put so much emphasis on the dictum "Know Thyself." Even those who temperamentally find it easy to pass by the implications of this idea are probably going to agree that Socrates was talking about something more than your taste in movies and your limit for drinks. Just how deep an issue he is addressing, and how to explore it, is up to each of us to decide individually.

For the second point I turn to the New Testament, which, along with patriotism, has unfortunately become one of the last refuges of scoundrels. Using the Bible to make a case for one's closely held point of view is a national sport, and I am absolutely not interested in adding to the debate. I would like only to point out one particular quote attributed to Jesus, the guy with ultimate street cred in America. He apparently said, "Seek first the Kingdom of Heaven, and all else will be added unto you." This story, messy as it is, is about that idealistic search.

As it unfolded, the search triggered extraordinary and overpowering experiences that were—as I found in trying to write about them—very difficult to describe. But I realize now that that problem comes with the territory. Actual exploration is never about places we have already visited and that lend themselves to easy description. As the poet Richard Wilbur wrote, "All that we do is touched with ocean, yet we remain on the shore of what we know."

This book is my best shot at describing a plunge into that ocean, and the heavy work of a lifetime: returning to a different, more heartfelt shore.

1.

It was around 2 a. m., the time I seemed to wake up during those few months, abruptly, watchful, with a feeling something between obedience and anticipation. After a string of cool days, the air in the house was chilly enough that I wrapped myself in the burgundy-and-black throw my mother had crocheted for me years before.

On that morning, in the fall of 1974, I stationed myself as usual, facing the picture windows of my little rental-on-a-hill in Redwood City, California, allowing me to keep company with the shimmering, uncountable lights of the Bay Area. They would be there when I opened my eyes, something beautiful to greet me.

I sat on the floor, cross-legged, with a couple of throw pillows under me. I kept my back straight, though my famously bad posture fought back as always. Being about as flexible as a floorboard, I had never been able to assume the more gymnastic, classical meditation position called the "lotus," or even its less demanding variation, the "half-lotus." Though the literature I had read agreed that those positions made it easier to sit for extended periods, I had long since decided that my physical limitations weren't going to stop me from diving deep into the practice of sitting meditation, however I could manage it.

I should have been lonely, I suppose. I went for days without seeing or speaking to anyone, including my girlfriend Jess. When we talked on the phone, I could hear how wary she had become of my growing preference for solitude. She sensed I wasn't fending off isolation—I was embracing it.

As had been the case for a few weeks, I didn't do any of the usual meditative practices I had learned from my reading. The mantra, the visualizations—all of it had drifted away. I didn't try to "do" anything. I was just watching, keeping a vigil without knowing what I was waiting for. It was wonderfully peaceful. There were no bad rock n' roll songs in my head, no critiques of myself or the world in general. There was a slow-mo character to my thinking, as if I were a pool of water that had always had a steady torrent flowing through it, but was suddenly mirror-placid except for a cupful of water tossed in at random intervals. There would be silence in my mind for a few minutes, and then a thought. Maybe "This is strange." Then silence again.

Because of my make-do, awkward sitting technique, the strain on my hips and back had become a reliable alarm, insisting after about an hour that I open my eyes and relax my position. But on this particular morning, I brushed past it. I held my position, ignoring my trembling muscles. In spite of the chilly early morning air, it wasn't long before rivulets of sweat slid down my face and back. My few thoughts were erased by the clarity and intensity of the pain. I didn't see this as any sort of self-punishment or solitaire version of S&M, but more as a demonstration of dedication to a path I had chosen for myself.

My steely determination didn't allow for even a faint awareness of the profound influences that held me there; that realization would be a long time in coming. When it finally arrived, it would not only be acknowledgement of the influences themselves, but of just how ruthlessly I had buried them, in an unmarked grave, deep inside.

A few thoughts punched their way through the burning, saying: Why not sit here a little longer? Just a little. The pain is nothing but resistance to being here, right now. Just muscles that can't surrender their memories. Why keep running away? Why not let yourself be here?

So I kept going. There was finally nothing left but sheer stubborn will: no "meditating," no watching, no equanimity—and certainly no deeper questions about how I could withstand such pain, much less why I would invite it in the first place. I could feel my t-shirt sticking to my chest, my hair plastered to my forehead. Everything fell away; I concentrated on the act of breathing.

Time went by, my muscles alternating between periods of violent shaking and steady, implacable tension. I heard only a constant hissing sound—the flow of blood sounding in my ears?—which eventually became a much louder ringing noise. There was a snatch of Gregorian chant that morphed into the sound of a crowd of people, murmuring and shuffling through a large hall, then amplified and sharpened into the sound

6

of children on a playground. Emerging from that noise, cutting through it, was a single voice that I knew well: my mother's. I heard her calling me, the way she often did at the end of long summer days, when it was time for supper and I was outside playing. I felt a surge of affection for her, and I answered silently, wanting to reassure her. I'm here, mom! Over here! I'm fine! I'm doing just fine!

My thoughts came back at me then, harshly. What did I think I was doing? This was sick. No one in his right mind would do any of this. Did I imagine this was how Francis of Assisi got his start?

Sarcasm was always a strong suit for me. In the world as I had known it, barbed self-criticism was an art form.

I felt myself splitting open. Not just that the muscles in my hips were about to be ripped apart like pulled pork, but that something was opening in my heart and mind, expanding in a startling way. Then, in an urgent tone, a thought came: "Be born. Be born." The air became thick with some kind of powerful nostalgia and empathy—was it compassion? Whatever it was, the stuff vibrated in me like a bow stroke on a cello. "Be born. Be born." And I nodded my head, sweat dropping from my eyebrows to my cheeks.

I raised my right hand and laid my fingers gently on my sweaty temple. Even more gently and slowly, I cupped my cheek in my hand. The gesture was tender and loving, completely acknowledging the strange and dangerous seas I was sailing. It wasn't judging whether I was crazy or not, wasn't trying to make something happen. It was totally supportive, the kind of touch that I had only rarely experienced from anyone, and certainly not from myself. When I put my hand on my face it was usually rough and unthinking, like scratching an itch, or rubbing my eyes. This was something very different.

When I finally broke my position, the flood of relief I felt was tinged with disappointment. There was something left undone, a place I had not gone yet.

After a few hours of sleep, as the sun was coming up, I did my series of yoga postures followed by more sitting. Then, the usual stirrings of thoughts about food. They were noisier than ever that morning, because my fasting had become increasingly severe. Why not a decent breakfast? Why are you doing this, what's the point? It's masochistic. The answer that emerged was: "Millions of people around the world are starving today, and the least I can do is to share a little solidarity with them." Even then I was aware it was more complicated than this. Eating issues always are.

I had only a mug of tea that morning, and by lunchtime my stomach was cramping and contracting; I paused often to take slow, deep breaths. I had learned that deep breathing was important around what would have been normal meal times, when a kind of automatic anticipation of food kicked in. Hungry as I was, I naturally felt a surge of desire to bolt the food even as I was preparing it. But the stronger the drive, the more I resisted, the more I stood back and marveled at it. Just look how *desperate* I am for this food! Deep breathing pulled the plug on my almost panicky sense of urgency.

That afternoon, I ate a piece of toast with avocado and melted cheese on it. Sitting at the table, I handled knife and fork gently. I cut a small corner, chewed it slowly, waiting fifteen seconds or so after swallowing before repeating the process. It took a long time to eat. But I had time.

I had quit my miserable liquor store job two weeks before. It was the second miserable liquor store job of my short working life, and the interval that separated the two—a year spent in France, working for Stanford University—had by contrast made that second job even more depressing than the first. I knew with certainty it was time to leave when, after a little more than a year, I finished my sitting practices one morning and realized the only reason I was going to work was that I needed the money. There was nothing else to it, and it just wasn't enough.

At the end of my last day, I came home feeling elated and rock-solid about my decision. I had very little money saved—about eight hundred dollars—but it didn't matter. As I sat on my cushions that night, in the dark early hours, I knew what it felt like to do the right thing, the harmonious thing. Not necessarily the exciting thing, or the outrageous and daring thing, or even the moral thing—though it might or might not have been all of those—but the thing that felt genuine. It was a moment so sweet and luminous that I just wasn't used to it.

With time on my hands, I began to do yoga and sitting three times a day. If I ate at all, it was two small meals, one in the morning and one in late afternoon. It was a routine, but one that was new every day, each moment arriving slowly and gently, loaded with possibilities. Simple things delighted me: sunlight through windows, the taste of tea, the soft touch on my cheek of air in motion. I bought a few cheap art supplies—a simple set of ten watercolors with some brushes and a watercolor pad, some bottles of India ink. I painted unremarkable craggy landscapes and views of lakes and forests, constantly fascinated by the process, especially the various effects of watercolor.

Then there were my afternoon walks, wandering the streets of the hills above the bay, past endless rows of trim tract houses to outlying neighborhoods of weathered, overgrown bungalows bracketed by empty fields of anonymous dry brush. At first for an hour, later for two or three hours at a time, I was never sure why I walked. For exercise? Okay. To explore the area? I guess. I never thought of it as meditation or therapy or as anything other than "taking a walk," but it became a powerful force.

Leaving my house felt like a launch into deep space. I never knew where I would go until I got to the next corner. The sound of my own footsteps, a car horn in the distance, the sight of the rows of wonderful magnolias lining the streets—all of it became a sort of communing, something I took in very deliberately. I was often brought up short by the realization that my experience of what was around me had always been so second-hand. I had been taught to learn just enough to allow me to categorize and dismiss everything I encountered, to stop wondering and get on to the next thing. The walks encouraged me to go back and learn how to use my senses all over again, as if I were a child.

It was amazing I found my way home every day.

Just a few weeks later, I found myself sitting on the floor of a lecture hall at Lone Mountain College in San Francisco, along with about a hundred other people, doing a guided meditation led by a bearded, saffron-robed Sufi master. It was unlikely on many levels, but most especially because of my bedrock ferocious desire to be alone in whatever my interior explorations were. I saw organized religion—especially Roman Catholicism, the brand I had smoked for many years—as toxic. I didn't even like the word "meditation," really; it was just too loaded. It conjured up images of Asian people with shaved heads and flowing robes, all of which reeked of organized religion.

The room was cool and musty-smelling. The only sound to be heard, other than the speaker's voice and an occasional cough from somewhere in the group, was the ticking, tapping noises from a couple of old radiators in opposite corners.

Having brought my cushions from home, sitting on that floor was a familiar experience, one that brought with it the familiar buildup of strain in my hips, the screaming tension in my back and neck. After listening to nearly two hours of guided meditation and reflections on mysticism, I had to keep my eyes closed. The act of looking at anything sapped too much energy from the effort to cope with the raging of my body. Some familiar, scathing, self-critical thoughts contended with the refined voice of the Sufi master, but even those were dying out in my personal furnace.

I did some deep breathing. It wasn't as if I couldn't change my position or abandon it completely. We weren't being monitored, as is done in strict, regimented sitting practices like Japanese zazen. But I had decided—in this familiar cold sweat, in this mad, stubborn overdrive that was now so familiar to me—that I wouldn't budge until the talk was over.

As the minutes crawled by, I found myself praying he would finish. When finally he paused for a long moment, I thought I was saved. Instead, I heard him say: "Now I am going to pass into the consciousness of each one of you."

2.

There is a lyric about family in Tim Minchin's song "White Wine in the Sun" which says, "These are the people who make you feel safe in this world." When I first heard this, at age sixty-three, I finally realized the truth: As I grew up, there were no people who made me feel safe in the world.

On my first day of school in 1955, I sat at my desk and wept silently. It didn't help much to notice I wasn't alone; more than a few of the fifty-eight kids in that first grade classroom were crying, too. Sister Constance Mary did her best to put us at ease.

"Why are you crying? Do I look like a bear who's going to eat you? Grraaaahhh!" She waved her arms and flashed her teeth, drawing a nervous laugh from us. It would take some time to settle in with this person who seemed a lot like a woman, but couldn't possibly be one. This strange impish face peering out at me from stiff white headgear covered with a head-to-toe cascade of black. Black. It was worrisome. So unlike anything else in the world.

She distributed a box of Binney & Smith crayons to each of us ("Eight Different Brilliant Colors!"), along with a single sheet of paper that smelled of some sort of medicine and bore the simple lines of a page from a coloring book. It was a picture of a fight. One figure— long hair, fluffy wings, serene expression—was clad in knee-high tunic and breastplate, and stood tall with sword poised to strike. The other was falling, shielding its horned head with its arms, its bat-like wings collapsing under it.

I was more at ease now, coloring. I knew how this worked. It was a relief to have something to concentrate on. I was good at staying inside the lines.

Sister explained the story of Saint Michael and Lucifer, the great battle between loyal angels and demons, between Light and Darkness. She told us details about heaven and hell, and about our own role in the battle, our duty to see that good prevails.

It was fun to color St. Michael—a light touch of blue for his wings, yellow for his hair. Lucifer was less fun, mostly because the color choices were limited, as far as I could see. Red was useful, black was inevitable. There was that black again.

So much happened in that first month. I learned to crowd myself into my desk seat to make room for my Guardian Angel, the celestial friend who would help me do the right thing when I might be tempted otherwise. When the bell rang on the half-hour, I learned to stop whatever I was doing and, in unison with my classmates, chant the invocation: "Sacred Heart of Jesus, all for Thee, Jesus, Mary, Joseph." Most important of all, I learned to adopt a facial expression that was blank but attentive. It was cover for the fear that blossomed in me like a black flower. When you are being given answers to deep questions about life, questions you have not yet been able to formulate for yourself, it's easy to be frightened. The world looks too big, too overwhelming, too soon.

Sister tossed shocking stories at us, waiting for our oohs and aahs. Most were about Jesus, and they not only justified my fear, they amplified it. If the best person imaginable could be seized by a mob, tortured and horribly murdered, there was no way to claim that the earth was a nice place. It was impossible to be too cautious in such a world. It was like living in a horror movie where, though nothing overtly violent has happened yet, you fully expect it. The musical score might ebb and flow, but it is always ominous.

On the playground at lunchtime, was it reasonable to laugh? To feel exhilaration, playing kickball? Not really. In a world like this, all forays into "fun" were less like enjoyable activities and more like desperate, jagged bursts of energy, what-the-hell attempts to outrun a reality that would settle back in once the fun was over.

I noticed Jesus never laughed. Nobody around him laughed. Being savior of the world was serious business. When I looked at the crucifix above the classroom door, or at the painting of his bloody body on the cross, bearing the inscription, "Greater Love Than This, No Man Hath," I got the message. Still, in spite of myself, I laughed sometimes.

I needed to love Jesus, Sister said. Of course I did. But as a stern requirement it got a response about as spontaneous as a catechism recitation. How to love someone you don't know? How to love someone you *do* know? How to love someone who is all-powerful and who appears willing to use that power to crush you like a bug? It's a situation that makes it a little hard to relax.

Coming home in the afternoon, my mother would say, "How was school?" And: "Have a pomegranate. Eat it over the sink." She was often pre-occupied, somewhere else, simmering. I didn't want to notice this, fearing I might be its cause. I didn't want to know what was cooking her, but I might have guessed: my father. Had I chosen to look, I might have noticed that they were not friends.

My father usually appeared just before my sister and I were sent to bed. More pre-occupied even than my mother, he cut a stern figure: sharp jaw and chin, thin lips, cigarette smoke. A tall scotch-and-water was his first order of business, Cutty Sark or J&B. He was not big on physical affection. As a TV writer and producer, he provided us a comfortable life, even if he himself never seemed comfortable. Living as we did, in a large house with a pool, in a prosperous part of L.A.'s San Fernando Valley; the major obstacle to acquiring anything was not money but the annoying amount of time it took to go out and get it. To be anxious or unhappy seemed ungrateful.

Into the winter months, Sister kept up a steady stream of stories. She talked about saints now, their miracles and triumphs, their unswerving love of Jesus. She insisted that we talk to them and ask for help in times of trouble, that we admire and even emulate them. If I accepted what she said, it was only because her ideas laid claim to the empty space inside, lodging in the deepest soft folds of the child brain. The stories towered over my small life, bathing everything in a somber shadow that was disturbing and frightening. In the urgent search for perspective, I told myself that maybe this was the meaning of growing up. Facing the truth about life. Maybe this was why grown-ups seemed so preoccupied, why my father was so stern, why my mother simmered. I never talked to them about any of it. There was little talk about God at home, but I knew He was important to my parents because, despite late hours on Saturday night with plenty of scotch flowing, my father still dragged out of bed every Sunday and hauled us to noon mass, brooding in the pew, dark glasses failing to disguise his mood.

Being introduced to the martyrs did not improve things. The very idea of martyrdom was a shock, though given the story of Jesus it should not have been. If His dad could allow Him to be tortured and killed, then anything was possible. Sister explained that even young people not much older than us had been slaughtered in gruesome ways for believing in Jesus. She posed the obvious question: Would we be able to die for Jesus? I was ashamed of my silent response, but it made me all the more determined to participate in this great project, this suffering for Jesus. It would have been unthinkable to refuse. It was a sacred obligation.

I began to look through my father's Sunday missal, frozen with fear and fascination by the full-color reproductions of paintings showing the scourging of Jesus, his bloody death on the cross, and the deaths of martyrs like Saint Stephen, stoned by a mob, and Saint Lawrence, roasted on a grill. This was how I finally fell hard, in love with suffering. Like most love, it was double-edged. Though it lodged inside me, a worm chewing at any sprouts of spontaneous joy, it did give life a doomed nobility. It shaped the drama of pain into that very small-bore gratification so familiar to practitioners of self-pity.

As satisfying as it was, the love of suffering never left me free of the feeling that I was a fraud.

Then came the bad part. The day I felt the wrath of Sister Constance Mary. It came from nowhere, violently, like an earthquake. One spring day in 1956, I sat on one of the long, warped lunch benches with my friend David Libby. He sang a little rhyme his dad had learned in the army, set to the tune of a song from Disney's *Snow White*. It made me laugh. As I repeated it, I felt myself being spun around, then lifted off the bench by my shirt front. Buttons popped and fell to the ground. Other students went silent, chewing their sandwiches and cookies, watching with heads down as Sister shook me.

"What did you say?" Teeth clenched, her smile was eerie, her impish features now demonic. My feet left the ground as she shook me and asked the question again.

I stammered, I said nothing. My mind, far out at sea, sent frantic distress signals, received by no one. She dragged me fifty feet to the gate of the convent garden, behind which I was at last blessedly invisible to my schoolmates. She sat me on a white stone bench, next to a birdbath featuring a small statue of a man with a stone bird perched on his extended stone arm.

I broke down. She looked at me coldly. "I'm going inside for lunch. When I come back, you're going to tell me what you said."

I sat on the bench for an eternal twenty minutes. My gasping, hiccupping sobs subsided. It didn't seem worth it to wipe my nose. The water in the birdbath was as murky as my thoughts, but a few things were obvious. I was being punished for being bad. I wanted to see my pain as martyrdom, but that was impossible. I was not suffering for God, and, anyway, Sister Constance Mary could not be an evil torturer. She was more like Saint Michael, and I the demon, falling back, cowering before a righteous anger. It had never occurred to me that I was bad enough to attract such punishment, but the evidence was undeniable. I briefly wondered what would happen to me, but then decided it didn't matter.

I repeated the song when Sister returned, going light and whispery on what seemed to me the most damaging parts:

> Whistle while you work
> Hitler is a jerk
> Who's a weenie is a peenie
> Now it doesn't work

Only much later did I learn that the third line was "Mussolini broke his weenie."

But that's a technicality.

With contempt oozing from her face, she moved in close and recited the magic incantation that would change my life, though no one would ever remark a be-fore-and-after difference.

"You're a dirty boy, Paul."

By then, I knew this was true; but hearing her say it aloud put an official seal on the horror and shame of it.

She went on to tell me I needed to apologize to Jesus. Though I agreed, I could not see that it would matter much. When you're dirty, what could possibly change that? If you are like a cheap toy that is defective right out of the box, apologies are meaningless. There is no fix, there is only the scrap heap.

Back in class that afternoon, I sat at my desk, burning with the horror of my new truth. Sister showed no sign of what had happened. Was she just moving on from a situation that could not be salvaged? Or was the whole thing so insignificant that she had already forgotten it? The latter seemed impossible.

I braced for a serious scolding at home, but none came. There was only an off-handed remark by my mother, who laughingly said the school nurse had called her about my "deportment problem." "I guess your teacher didn't want to call me herself," she chuckled. "She got Mrs. Dodd to do her dirty work for her."

I was relieved. Even my parents would not call out my shame.

3.

It is an exquisitely Kafka-esque nightmare to be the defendant in a courtroom lodged somewhere deep inside you, at a never-ending trial where you are also the extremely effective prosecutor and the cowed, timid defense attorney. But that is the reality I lived with, a constant presence that hovered like a wraith at the edges of my conscious thinking.

It is completely sensible to ask how a single event, my encounter with Sister Constance Mary, could exact such a toll. It has to be true that many other children walk away from similar events completely unscathed. My best shot at an answer is this: because of some twisted genetic formation or temperamental quirk, I was one of that group of Catholic kids who in dead earnest swallows every commandment, every Bible story, every teaching, every wacked-out word from the clerical mouth. For us, life is early on defined in terms of Good and Evil, requiring a constant parsing of our thoughts and actions. And when cathedral-sized scruples are tuning in to the most miniature flaws, in yourself or in others, it tends to keep you very busy, though maybe not so happy.

What happens as a few years go by? You might become obsessive-compulsive, hyper-critical, or just an introspective control freak; but there is no doubt that when you hear the authorities tell you that God loves you, you'll have no idea what they're talking about. You are far too busy keeping score.

The first order of business for someone like me was to create a façade that would provide cover for the defendant and his off-the-charts shame, a mask that would offer the world a convincing if counterfeit Golden Boy image. It turned out that this was something I could do. Perennial class president, excellent student, altar boy who offered to serve at the poorly-attended 6:30 a.m. weekday mass. But if I managed to be popular among my classmates and the neighborhood kids, my parents didn't seem to buy into my performance. It wasn't so much that I wasn't convincing, but more that they were not very attentive. They were an impossibly tough audience for all three of their children, if only because they were so absorbed by their long, twilight battle with each other, the vengeful, tit-for-tat war of attrition that bound them together for a lifetime. It didn't leave them with a lot of energy for kids. What was available was most often the cool, understated approval of high expectations. It was hard to get warm standing around the fire of our familial affection.

Like most long feuds, its causes were bound up with the strikes and counter-strikes that gave it momentum over many years. Also like most long feuds, it was painfully boring, finally, to anyone but the two combatants.

Its origins lay with my father's occasional infidelities, and his much more frequent dalliances with alcohol. Because he was lord of the kingdom, my mother was driven to play a tough defensive game, one that augmented her icy disgust with various threats, such as exposing his sins to the Catholic community whose approval he cherished. In rare moments, her threats involved actually leaving him, but those few were not acted upon.

There was never any quarter given, and none asked.

The one area where my Golden Boy façade was especially unconvincing to my parents and everyone else was athletics. There was no hiding the fact that, aside from being a decent if uninspired swimmer, I was a klutz. This bothered my mother certainly, but was a far greater disappointment to my father. There was irony in this, given his own positively scrawny, stooped frame and his refusal to participate in any sports beyond an infrequent set of tennis.

What was odd about his tennis playing, aside from its being a rare event, was its mad intensity. In his late forties, at the only similar family outing I can recall, he served with such ferocity that he burst masses of blood vessels in his shoulder and chest. He seemed almost proud as he took off his shirt to display his blotchy, purple wounds.

This was just one of many moments when my father revealed himself as a full-tilt maniac. Someone who could set in motion his personal drives without always being able to find the "off" switch. A man who when sitting up all night at his desk in his upstairs office trying to finish a script might nod off and fall to the floor with a reverberating thud, but who would then get right back up in his chair and try to continue.

In some ways, it was not surprising that this person would be terribly disappointed in a son who as a Little Leaguer seemed so lost, so awkward and tentative out there on the lonely steppes of right field. But beyond his disappointment, I wonder still whether he noticed flashes of his own character in his son, variations of his own drives. How could he have missed them? At age seven, when I learned to play solitaire, I sometimes played for an entire day. There was the summer when I turned nine, too. My father —this man whom I never saw swim even one complete lap in our pool—decided he would be my "swimming coach." His plan was that I start out swimming ten laps and increase that number by two every day. He made up two sets of flash cards that he would hold up to let me know how many laps I had done and my time on each lap. After just five days, when I should have stopped at twenty laps, I waved him off and kept swimming. I swam with nothing but determination in my head, with no thought about laps or times or anything else. I stopped only when my arms refused the commands of my mind, when I was too dizzy to swim in a straight line. I had completed a hundred and two laps.

At the age of twelve I ran full speed into the further complications of male Catholic puberty and its cruel overlord, the sacrament of Penance. (Once known as Confession, these days it is called Reconciliation. You say tomahto.) Entering the pitch black little closet, I would kneel down and wait for the opaque, amber-colored plastic screen to slide open, signaling that I was to begin listing my crimes. This was the moment when I had to admit to God that I had disappointed Him, and the Irish priests who were the intermediaries in this were none too gentle about calling me down. I quickly discovered I could never, ever confess to masturbation, when one of the fathers unleashed a loud and vehement condemnation of my "impure thoughts," which I had confessed as a kind of trial balloon. You know: you have to find out the limits of the Truly Bad. I exited the confessional secure in the knowledge that masturbation was on the far side of the limit. I was absolutely sure my entire class had heard every indignant word he shouted at me, as they knelt in the pews outside the confessional. I was not just condemned, but mortified, too.

Then began the nasty tangle of "sacrilegious" behavior that my rule-crazed brain cooked up for me. It went like this: Go to confession but don't confess masturbation. That constitutes a "bad confession" in which I have knowingly left something out. Then I receive Holy Communion after a bad confession, which is a sacrilege, a mortal sin which damns me forever. Next confession, I don't confess masturbation *or* the terrible sacrilege, and that's a double sacrilege—something worse than eternal damnation. Difficult, but I was sure I had done it. I could imagine the mortal sins piling up on my soul like black flapjacks. It might be hard to accept that anyone could take all of this seriously. You have to try. Isolated as I was in my shame and my certainty that I was the only one going through this, I saw no other reality. It was only many years later that I discovered there were boys my age who got together for masturbation contests to see who could shoot farthest.

Who knew?

My inevitable rebellion finally came at age nineteen. It was modest, but powerful enough to propel me into the ranks of Fallen Away Catholics, as opposed to being one of those who continued to follow Church teachings and practices after having had his faith "tested." My faith, such as it was, had been weakened by various encounters with angry, bitter nuns, beginning—spectacularly—with Constance Mary, and continuing in high school, with disturbingly chummy old Jesuit priests with serious untreated dandruff problems and terrible breath. I also had studied enough about the world to realize I might just as easily have been born in another place, with slightly darker skin, a five syllable surname, and a fierce devotion to Ram and Krishna.

The event that finally shook me loose from the fold was a midnight Christmas mass in 1968. As usual, I went to our local parish church with my parents, my sister, and brother. It was another in a series of big productions, with loads of evergreens and candles, along with a virtually professional choir directed by a Hollywood movie composer. This was Los Angeles's San Fernando Valley, after all. I continued my own private tradition of stubbornly ignoring the awful leaden quality of the whole exercise, which always left me feeling heartsick. At the time, we all conspired in trying to make this charade warm and wonderful; and I might have been able to do it again had it not been for Father Fahey.

Father Fahey was the pastor of the parish, and always the midnight mass celebrant. Irish- born, with silver mane, thick brogue, and gin blossoms all over those generous cheeks, he was as hale and boisterous as he could manage while being clearly mystified by the customs of the natives in the strange foreign land of Southern California.

From the moment he came into the sanctuary, preceded by the altar boys, I knew—we all knew—something was wrong. There was a hitch in his step, a hesitation and a sudden lurch when he first knelt on the altar steps. But it was when he read the Epistle that all doubt was removed: he was drunk. Theatrically impassioned for a moment, fumbling and lost the next. "Beloved: The grace of God our Savior has appeared to ALL MEN," his voice rose and echoed in the silence of the church. "Instructing us, in order that, rejecting ungodliness and wordless—mmm, worldluss—WORLDLY LUSTS…" A spray of saliva shone in the bright light for a moment. He glared around him, seeming to dare anyone to take up the cause of lust. He muttered to himself as he tried to find his place in the text. "Glory be…glory, glory be…ah, shite."

When he mounted to the pulpit to deliver his sermon, my rage and embarrassment (embarrassed for *him*!) were making me squirm. Wasn't anybody going to stop this terrible charade? I mean, before he puked in the sanctuary? Yet no one moved, no one objected. Some eyes met, expressing puzzlement or disapproval; most stayed on their prayer books. I noticed I was just another member of a congregation conspiring to use its collective will to make this scene go away. I hated all these people around me, these gutless toadies; I hated myself. My mother sat reverently, with downcast eyes and serious expression. My father was busy rearranging

27

the placemark ribbons in his Saint Joseph Daily Missal (with Italian leather cover).

I stood up. I avoided the eyes of my family as I stepped past them to reach the aisle. When I got outside and felt the cold air on my face, I realized I had been holding my breath. I was shivering, probably more from anger than cold.

This was one of those rare moments when I could say without a doubt what I did *not* want. There seemed no hope of my ever knowing what I actually did want, but this negative form was good enough for the moment. That night I could finally inch my way out to the far reaches of my mind's borders and stand teetering on the edge of the blackest chasm in the universe, shake my fist at deep space and scream, "Fuck you, You Bastard! You can keep your Heaven. After all the Catholic shit I have been through, I'm not *interested* anymore. If Hell is home to uglier, cruder hypocrisy than this, I'm kind of curious!"

In hindsight, an unfortunate bit of bravado.

4.

In the spring of 1970, as a third year undergraduate, four years before I would learn much of anything about eastern religions, I managed to get myself arrested. It happened at a sit-in demonstration against the American invasion of Cambodia that had been ordered by Richard Nixon just days before. Nixon's move, seen as an expansion of the Vietnam War, was met with instant outrage on college campuses across the country. At Stanford, where I was, there were a couple of nights of burning cars and vandalized buildings, which in turn triggered non-violent alternative protests that attempted to shut down the university to avoid more violence. It was at one of these sit-ins, where about fifty students blocked the entrance of the administration building, that I was singled out for arrest. Probably because I was talking too much to the two Santa Clara County sheriffs who had ordered us to disperse. But, you see, I wanted to *explain* our position to them, to enlist them, make them understand why we were the *good guys*.

They were unimpressed. I was pulled to my feet,

handcuffed, and put into the back seat of a waiting patrol car. It became a circus. The students surrounded the car and sat down, chanting "We love you." Someone let the air out of the tires. The sheriffs called for backup.

I was in shock, of course, as I sat there, dressed in my neat bell bottoms and corduroy sport coat. I was not some rabble-rousing hippie, God no. I was far too conventional for that. All that long greasy hair, the scruffy beards, the shredded jeans, the patchouli oil? Ick. Free love, maybe. But poor hygiene? Never.

When the Tactical Squad arrived, with their shields and truncheons and their diplomacy-free attitude, the students were quick to scatter. I was dragged to another squad car, one with fully inflated tires, and driven to the Stanford Firehouse, which was being used as a temporary holding pen for any arrests made that day. As I sat handcuffed to a chair, I was by turns fuming and amused, as you might expect a child of privilege to be in such a situation. How dare they arrest someone who suffered through five years of Little League, who had been an altar boy and student body president of his Catholic high school? So I was now the Enemy of the State? Hmmph. But the experience was frightening, too. And I knew it would be messy. I would have to rely on my parents in navigating unknown twists and turns of the court system I would soon be enmeshed in. Luckily, that morning, four of us members of the sit-in demonstration group had tossed $200 each into a contingency bail fund which we left at our apartment, so I spent only about four hours without my belt and shoes in a county jail cell before I was rescued.

What completely escaped my attention at the time

was the odd pleasure and satisfaction I took from the experience. Many years would pass before I would catch a glimpse of that response and be able to identify it for what it was: the martyr realizing his fondest dream. It was a cheap, fifty-cent version of martyrdom, true, but even in its laughably dilute form the essential ingredients were there. I was the advocate of an unimpeachable cause, misunderstood, unjustly singled out, and persecuted by the authorities. I was now on the right side of the fence, among the flock of the righteous who are wrongly punished, as opposed to being the six-year-old sinner who had been condemned by God and Sister Constance Mary so many years before.

The truth was that, as a draft-age male in the Vietnam War era, my entire life was a kind of Martyrdom Lite. The war was a disaster, obviously, a misbegotten adventure from the beginning, and I was clear about not participating in it. But if I wasn't going to allow myself to be drafted, there were only a few other options: I could go to graduate school and get another draft deferment, I could flee to Canada, or I could go to jail. The very idea of any kind of graduate work—more of the interminable academic drudgery I had come to hate—was almost as unbearable as exile in a freezing climate, so I told my parents I was planning to go to jail. Did I mean it? Probably not. But my decision had that whiff of doomed, misunderstood nobility that in my unconscious mind would make my suffering more than just the fallout from a young man's self-destructive choice.

After graduation, I retired to my parents' new home in Malibu, where they had moved as the San Fernando Valley had become more and more crowded. I was bitter and moody, waiting for the draft notice that I was sure would come. I played pool. I read books: Nikos Kazantzakis, Walker Percy, Karl Jaspers. I ran on the beach every morning before the sun came up. I talked on the phone with my girlfriend Iris, who had graduated with me and was back at her parents' house in Mountain View, near Stanford, while she contemplated her next move. I tried to ignore the news, to avoid any word about the war. It was all too depressing.

And then, in December, I got a call from one of my friends from the non-violent protest group. He congratulated me on getting out from under the draft. I was indignant. How could he joke about something so touchy? It was a technicality, he said, but as good as a Get Out of Jail Free card: every month, the Secretary of Defense "called up" a certain number of young men from the draft pool, and since that number had been zero for the six months following my eligibility (which was my graduation day), I was dropped from the system.

The feeling of relief was better even than Martyrdom Lite. I was free.

Within a month, I was back in Northern California. I moved into an East Palo Alto apartment that Iris and I shared with a graduate student couple, friends of friends. Because the notion of returning to school was so nauseating, I took that first terrible job, stocking shelves and standing behind the register at a liquor store; soul-killing work that I tolerated only because I was so infatuated with the world of fine wine that I would have done practically anything to become even an irrelevant part of it. The greater part of my time at the store, ringing up candy bars and half-gallons of cheap bourbon, was not what I had in mind; and certainly not what my parents—who had spent lots of money on my education—had in mind, either. My mother's initially casual mentions of law school became increasingly pointed.

The drudgery of the job, the $90-a-week salary, the passive-aggressive battles with Iris, all of it contributed to the stern realization that the threat of the draft had only been the frying pan—this was the fire. As I soldiered through the first few months of 1972, my mood was increasingly dark. It was what I saw as the sheer profanity of my surroundings that helped to create an unrelieved burden, a weight on my chest. Not just my job, but the blaring signage of businesses along El Camino Real, the billboards, the radio noise, the exhaust of the cars, even the curbs and sidewalks with their forlorn snatches of weeds—all of it had an empty, abandoned feel I couldn't escape. In my mind, that same desert extended forever in all directions. There was nothing else.

Except wine, oddly enough. French wine in particular held magic for me, far more than the wines of other countries or even those made little more than an hour's drive from my apartment: in Napa, Sonoma, and other North Bay counties. I was hopelessly infatuated with the history, the lore, the tradition of wines from France's greatest growing regions. The misery of my job was suspended whenever I was handling these bottles—reverently opening a new pinewood case or admiring the refined, ornate labels as I stocked the shelves. It was painful not to be able to afford any of them, but for the moment it was enough to read as much as I could about them, and to bask in their aura like a lovesick, nerdy student sitting in class next to a gorgeous cheerleader.

The truth was, I had been a hopeless Francophile from age fourteen, when I first heard a native speaker recite a poem in French. I don't remember the poem, but I certainly remember the elegant sound and flow of the words. It was impossibly beautiful, like spoken music. As if the air that a French-speaker breathed was a rich, luscious dessert. At that moment, I told myself I would learn to speak French exactly like that. Though now after more than fifty years I have had to acknowledge only qualified success, it was not for lack of trying.

This was the upside of being impressionable and dreamy: being always open to the touch of magic, the flight of imagination, the unexpected shot of exhilaration that sometimes accompanies an idea. The downside was the vulnerability, the insecurity, the thin emotional armor easily pierced by sudden shocks that others would hardly notice. It was as if some physiological curse had placed my nerve endings too close to the surface of my skin.

I lived a routine which was as comfortable as it could be, given the carefully cultivated absence of any future plans, and of course a lack of money. In retrospect, our poverty was the blessing that prevented excesses we gladly would have indulged in. My girlfriend Iris and I shared the apartment with Leo, a doctoral candidate and amateur chef, as generously proportioned as I was thin, enthusiastic and skilled enough as a cook to encourage me in spending nearly all my disposable income on wine and food, as he did. His girlfriend Jan was busy as a researcher in Stanford's chemistry department, busy enough that it took her almost a year to discover that Leo was gay.

Iris was smarter than I was, but had also chosen an entry-level retail sales job—in a department store—as her first step after getting her diploma. I don't think she had the attachment to fashion that I had to wine; my guess was, she moved in with me because of my seeming helplessness. It brought out the mother in her. Either that or the fact that her mother, upon meeting me, had declared, "He looks just like Chopin!" This was true only in the sense that I looked haunted and consumptive most of the time.

What would break up our little household, and ultimately lead me to that pivotal moment, the Sufi master's talk at Lone Mountain College in 1974, was a visit from my friend Dan Moynier. Dan was an MBA student who carried with him a huge whiff of counterculture. He was always giving me liberal amounts of advice, literature, and marijuana. In February of 1972, he gave me a strange-looking, square, purple paperback book called *Be Here Now*. I thanked him and put it on my nightstand. It would be more than a month before I finally opened it. When I did, it changed everything.

For those unfamiliar with the book, it could be described as a popularizing of basic Buddhist and Hindu teachings, transmitted through an American Jew. Of course that description doesn't do it justice. It's like saying Bette Davis was an actress. What made the book extraordinary for me, and I suspect for many others of my generation, was that it contained some real "juice." There was actual energy and power in it, as opposed to the kind of dry, academic works I was accustomed to seeing. In breathtaking swings, from poetry to metaphysics to wry hipster humor, it swept away the major unspoken assumptions of the culture most of us live in, and it did it without rancor or thundering jeremiads. It said: "If we're not in the Here and Now, no matter how much food we put in our bellies, it's never going to be enough, and that's the feeling of Western man: he's got it all going in as fast as he can shovel it, he's got every sensual gratification he can possibly desire and *it's not enough*, because there's no Here & Now-ness about it."

The book was a powerful unspoken rebuke to childish, cartoonish visions of faith and religion. It shattered, or at least made a large dent in, the particularly nasty version of Catholicism I had concocted with the help of my fourteen years of Catholic schooling. It spoke with much greater heart and authority than any of the books or people that populated my youth. It was my first conscious encounter with Validity, rock-solid truth that went beyond my thoughts.

Its impact was in direct proportion to the terrible sense of drift, melodramatic stoicism, and sheer "lostness" gifted to me by the "adult" world. Not only did my mentors not know what life was; they were bent on making me use their set of rationalizations to get through it. This was the source of much misery. At any of the scotch-soaked celebrations my parents hosted, I would inevitably be snared by one or another unsteady glance and told: "God'll forgive you, but the tax man won't." Or: "Take a bite outta life before the other guy knows he's hungry." And especially: "You young rapist! For Chrissake, just don't get 'em pregnant."

I spent some time being angry, naturally, when I realized that I was taking religion much more seriously than the people who had sold it to me originally. Yet I couldn't stay in that spot too long either, just because of the message of the book. It was asking: What's keeping you from being here, right now, experiencing this moment completely? What are you holding onto? What grudge? What trauma? What crime? What obsession? What stash of stuff is so dramatic, so important, that you are willing to give up the current moment, which is essentially all there is anyway?

And then there was a message of particular interest for me: If you want to let all that dead weight go, you will even have to give up *your own sense of unworthiness*.

Now *that* would be a big job. My experience with Catholicism had pretty much marinated me in unworthiness.

Along with mind-boggling metaphysics, the book explained various practical things a person could do to become calmer, more aware, and happier. What a concept. None of this was ever part of my Catholic experience. It just wasn't in the playbook. Sanctifying grace, yes. The Sacraments, check. Original Sin was very big. But never really anything about how to find some balance and real contentment in life.

Catholicism, as packaged in the relative Dark Ages of the 1950s, was primarily concerned with frightening children enough to later make them frightened adults. Loyalty to abstractions was demanded, under pain of punishment from above. By contrast, the purple book laid out common sense guidelines for ethical behavior in work, family life, finances, and friendship—guidelines that provided their own feedback loop for personal satisfaction and fulfillment. Pretty attractive stuff. But here was the catch: my crypto-Catholic, hormone-laden mind turned out to be less attracted to blueprints for balance and contentment than to sections of the book that explained how to do various forms of yoga and sitting meditation. These were strange new frontiers, terra incognita that was crying out for exploration by a budding berserker, a kamikaze of introversion. The son of my father. Sitting cross-legged, stock-still on the floor seemed almost a recovered memory, tantalizingly obvious enough that the first dozen times I experimented with it, I found myself silently saying things like, "Right! Of course! This!" It seemed like an infinitely less distorted version of kneeling in a church pew as a child, doing an examination of conscience before confession, or, with face covered by open palms, searching for the correct language to use in talking with Jesus after Holy Communion.

Unfortunately, there was no section in the purple book about wine. I noticed this. The names of Grand Cru Burgundies were not going to appear anywhere in the Buddha's Four Noble Truths. This was to become the source of some of my most strenuous and elastic rationalizing in years to come.

5.

So, how to begin living this new life, trying to work with the revelations of the purple book? I didn't know what I was doing. But on the plus side, I didn't know what I was doing.

At the shop, I was more and more demoralized by endless hours spent ringing up beer and salami. As my mood deteriorated, lunch hour became a weird kind of purple-book-inspired refuge. After a ham on rye or roast beef on sourdough from Harry's Hofbrau, I would go into the back warehouse—badly lit and cool no matter the season—and position myself, cross-legged, eyes closed, on a stack of pinewood cases of 1966 Chateau Mouton-Rothschild. Surrounded by even higher stacks of other Classified Growth Bordeaux, Burgundies, Chablis, and Ports, I sat still for a half-hour or so. I tried out some of the purple book's techniques—watching my breath and mantra, mostly. I couldn't help but notice that because I was always busy churning out thoughts, I couldn't even conceive of exploring what made the machine tick. My curiosity now drove me to ask impossible questions that would not accept words as answers. What was this consciousness? What was it made of? What was it for? It was a new world that, once I had shrugged off some of the "Let's talk to God" baggage I had been carrying since childhood, became powerfully real to me.

By July, I was hard up against the dead-end nature of the job. I did have a modest cache of wine, of course, but that didn't seem to help much. I knew one of the owners of the shop wanted to get rid of me because I kept stumbling on places where he had stashed half-pints of bourbon to keep himself going during the day. I needed to get out, but there didn't seem to be choices. I had applied for some sales positions in wine wholesaling and been turned down for all of them.

Then I had another visit from my friend Dan. After we had smoked some of what he had brought, he asked if I had heard the news about Stanford's French overseas campus in the Loire Valley city of Tours. There was always a Resident Assistant living at the campus for a year or so, to help students with orientation, enrollment issues, field trips and such. The criteria for getting the job were, first, to have graduated from the university, and second, to have attended the overseas campus as a student. I was eligible, but had never given it a thought. He told me the person chosen to fill the spot in September had to drop out because of a family emergency. "You should get yourself over there and speak some French to 'em," he said.

They gave me the job.

I was ecstatic. I called my parents and told them the story. My mother, after a weighty silence: "Well.

It doesn't have much...direction, does it?" They were both ultimately supportive, but I am not so sure it wasn't because they knew I would do this even if they held their breaths and turned blue. At least they had the grace not to bring up the money they felt they had wasted on my education.

From the moment I arrived in France, though it wasn't completely clear at the time, everything was going to be about the purple book. It had done more than fire my imagination; it had touched some deep part of me that ached for recognition. It didn't matter whether I was reading in my apartment, sitting down to dinner with the students in the noisy dining room, or driving through the pastel landscapes of the Loire —there was only one issue. How was I going to find the peace, the equanimity of, say, the Buddha? I was so sick of all my moodiness, my sullen internal thumb-sucking, the flashes of unexplained rage. I felt constantly kicked around by envy and contempt, by the dull ache of inadequacy, by shame. Especially shame. The legacy of a backward education and my own particular brand of overscrupulousness.

There was huge attraction in even the razor-thin possibility I might be free of all of it. How could I not try, though the purple book told me in no uncertain terms that the very desire to be free would keep me from freedom? That I had to let it go to get it? Truly mad and maddening. The paradoxes were so juicy and frustrating, I was like a hunting dog, sniffing the air more and more urgently, whimpering as he catches a faint scent of the prey. I was oblivious to the fact that, as a child of western culture, I was making a contest out of Enlightenment—ready to goad, even taunt myself, if it meant a transformation would be possible.

My mind concocted parallel storylines for the year in France. I was not denying that it was about being a young man with an appetite for life, thrilled to find himself in an exotic but familiar country that he loved. That it was about his reveling in the sheer Frenchness of everything: the beauty of the countryside, the crooked rooflines of the villages, the storefronts, the alleys and boulevards, the cafes and churches, not to mention the food and wine. But beyond all that was another layer, one that insisted I had been plucked out of my familiar, comfortable, soporific environment and set down in this strange but dimly recognizable country in order to be alone. Not that I wouldn't be surrounded by people much of the time, but these were strangers, people with whom I had no bond, no history. I would be alone as I had never been before, and I felt this must be in order to allow me to do some work; work that only France and the purple book could cook up for me. I was certain I wasn't there simply to do my job as Assistant to the Directors, a.k.a. Registrar's Representative, Tour Guide, Hand-Holder, Occasional Translator. Nine to noon in the office, four days a week, with three weeks off at the end of each academic quarter? All that would never be more than a diversion.

I clung to that latter theory not just because it seemed true, but because I needed to crowd out the nagging competing narrative, that I was just a Young Temple of Testosterone looking for fun.

6.

Every day of that year held a built-in dilemma, a fresh collision of France's sensuality with the cosmic pronouncements of the purple book. Shall I go out and have roast duck for dinner, with a bottle of wine, maybe a nice Chinon? Sure, but don't forget that "you've tasted something somewhere in your past that's been so high, so much light, so much energy, that nothing you can experience through any of your senses or your thoughts can be enough! Somewhere inside, everybody knows that there is a place which is totally fulfilling. Not a desperate flick of fulfillment—it is a state of fulfillment."

You see the problem.

Whatever the purple book said, it was obvious I was never going to be some kind of self-anointed monk. As months went by, plenty of solid evidence piled up against that notion, including a messy sexual relationship with a student, something that was frowned upon by the administration and which ended only when the young woman in question finished her studies and returned to California. There was also a brainless, drunken afternoon which landed me in bed for two days. I had taken a little drive with a male student who was known to be a troublemaker, and ended up in a beautiful wooded area where we found an old hunters' shack, empty except for a cupboard containing five bottles of what turned out to be delicious white and rosé wines—all of which we drank.

In the past, I would have been protected from many such experiences by my reliably conventional nature, generally pretty ruthless in satisfying the expectations of others. But now, as I transitioned from social programming to freer, truer inner promptings inspired by the purple book, it was inevitable that I would sometimes—let's say often—conveniently mistake self-indulgent craziness for genuinely liberating action. When I misstepped and felt an accompanying jolt of angst, when I needed some way to confirm my dedication to the meditative path, there was thankfully a small collection of sayings from the purple book that created some breathing room around its fiery, urgent messages. The two I returned to most often when I needed to lick my wounds were, "When you know how to listen, everyone is your teacher," and "You've got to go at the rate you can go. You're finished with your desires at the rate you finish with your desires. You can't rip the skin off the snake. The snake must molt the skin."

So while still being deadly serious about the purple book, I could see even my most embarrassing foolishness as a kind of no-fault R&R. I knew I would return to the fray. I wasn't for a moment tempted to abandon this re-visioning of life, this work of interior spelunking. I couldn't give up because it felt unassailably, totally right and true, in a world where literally nothing else did. This was a departure from my usual way of approaching a daunting task; normally the slightest slip, the very first reverse, would cause me to give up. But in this work, there was no chance of that. It would be like giving up breathing.

The campus in France was a converted five-story apartment building with a stark gray stone exterior. Its cold, unadorned look was not at all what I had expected in France; it was more like what I imagined apartment buildings would look like in an affluent neighborhood in Minsk, or maybe Budapest. Its interior was equally spare and institutional, from the hollow echo of the granite-lined lobby, dominated by the smell of cleaning solvents, to tiny classrooms with tables covered in simulated wood contact paper, and the basement dining room with its collection of smells from past meals that refused to be forgotten.

One great asset the building did have, one that benefitted me very directly, was a terrific view of the Loire River, with its graceful stands of poplars and lush countryside. As if the large two-room layout of my apartment wasn't enough, it was also located on the building's fifth floor, overlooking a busy square and the river. And it had a balcony. Not some skimpy thing with wrought-iron railing and room for maybe a couple of plants, but a terrace, an esplanade of a balcony that extended a good fifteen feet from my door to the wall at its far edge, and ran nearly the whole length of my apartment. Sometimes in good weather I paced its length, back and forth, reading Ouspensky's *Tertium Organum* or Jack Kerouac's

Dharma Bums, like a priest reciting his breviary. When I was feeling playful, knowing no one could hear, I did impromptu De Gaulle imitations—nonsensical speeches delivered in a loud voice while looking out over the river below as if it were a sea of faces.

The apartment was sparsely furnished with mismatched, cast-off pieces, including a remarkably creaky old double bed. I began sleeping on the floor of my "living room," telling myself the old mattress would do my back no good. The bed wasn't really so bad, in truth, but I was determined to confront myself with this ascetic challenge, sleeping between two blankets, without a pillow. It was hard on my hips, shoulders, and neck, and made my rest shallow and intermittent for the first few months. Gradually I felt lighter when I awoke in the morning. My tense muscles had given way, just a bit, to the relentlessly firm floor. I liked the idea that gravity was forcing me to relax.

In retrospect, the austerity of the apartment was exactly the thing to plunge me further into my improvised spiritual practices. There was no TV, no music except what few cassette tapes I had brought with me, along with a small tape player that was on its last legs. Eclectic is a generous descriptor of the music. There was the original cast recording of *My Fair Lady*. There was Poulenc's piano concerto and the album *Fragile* by the progressive rock group, Yes. I even had Neil Diamond's cover of Leonard Cohen's "Suzanne." The selection was sparse enough that after a few months I found myself preferring silence.

Meanwhile, there was my job. Aside from bureaucratic scuffling and shuffling, it luckily offered me another role: unofficial orientation officer. I organized a wine tasting course for the students and took some of them with me to visit local winemakers. I led outings to some of the best restaurants in the area, including Chez Barrier, at the time a Michelin 3-star establishment. (One student offered the ultimate praise: "Everything tastes like steak!") Though I did it all with relish, genuinely loving every minute of it, somehow I would find myself back in my apartment asking, "What the hell was THAT?" These were the moments I fell back on the saying, "You have to go at the rate you can go. You can't rip the skin off the snake."

As winter approached, I felt the power of being alone in the late afternoon, when office hours were done and dinner was hours away. The time stretched out. Rain on my windows seemed loud and full of significance. I realized that no one particularly cared what I did or where I was, and I began to luxuriate in the sensation. There was a great lightness in feeling that I was not at that moment on anyone's radar, not part of anyone's plans or expectations. Not just alone in a room waiting for someone, or thinking about meeting someone later, but blissfully anonymous and even—strange to say it—non-existent. Seeing my own almost giddy response to this solitude was a big indicator to me of how burdened I had felt, how obligated, how beholden and responsible I had been to those who had surrounded me at home. That realization was elating, but disturbing, too. I was forced to try on a new self-description, very different from the one I had wishfully accepted until then: bright young fellow, thoughtful, independent spirit, mind of his own. The more likely scenario suddenly became: easily influenced, desperate to please, deeply conventional. It was not a pretty picture, but I couldn't turn away. It felt too much like a bulls-eye.

More seriously than ever, I followed the purple book's suggestions about sitting down, cross-legged on a cushion, for increasingly long periods. I was trying, as the book advocated, to watch my thoughts. Not to identify with them, not to judge them, but just to be open-endedly curious. I felt the desire to give witness to whatever was turbulent and mysterious in me.

Often my conclusion was, "Boy, am I shitty at this." But sitting finally made me aware that—as the purple book said—my previous way of looking at the world had been so absolute and certain, that I was *in prison.* Like most people, I had foregone conclusions for every occasion, ways to categorize experience and fit it into my world view. I knew how everything worked. But when what you already know describes the limits of the world you are willing to accept, that's a prison. And the thing about that kind of prison is: as long as you think you're in control and believe you're free, you can never get out.

Over time, I have learned that this is a near-constant challenge: how to accept and incorporate new and sometimes disturbing data into an established life view. It's basically the same problem the Catholic Church had in confronting Galileo. The Church had an inevitable investment in the status quo, and, well, isn't it just easier to deny the new data, and maybe even get out the thumb screws? This issue would become my predicament over the next few years, as increasingly unusual experiences followed in the wake of my meditation experiments.

When these arose, I validated and accepted them not because they fit into my world—they didn't—but because they were undeniably "real." As a child of good solid Western empiricism, I would certainly have rejected them if I could have. Though it was true that on some level I sought these new experiences, still this meditation stuff was the equivalent of tossing a lit match into the gas tank of my existing, coherent world.

There was another important bit of information I should have taken note of, too, which is that no matter how impressive a new, expanded life view might seem at first, it is not going to be the final destination, the Absolute End-All; not, as the purple book said, the "Big Ice Cream Cone in the Sky." It's just another waystation, another hypothesis, an updated view of the world, ready to be tested against yet another set of experiments in the ongoing lab of life. Like the scientific method, the process of human growth never ends. Unfortunately, this truth would escape me completely.

After a few more months, I had established a little routine for myself. After lunch I would go across the street to a local café called Le Musée, where I drank a hot *thé-citron* or sometimes a coffee, chatting with whichever students were there. In mid-afternoon, I came back to my apartment, where I would sit and read for an hour before doing my Hatha yoga postures and settling in for what I was finally willing to call "meditation."

It was a big surprise to me just how fiery many of those meditations became. The threat of consistent discipline made my mind wild with resistance; even the simple notion of watching my breath was enough to trigger a frantic, desperate, get-me-out-of-here response.

Thoughts tore through me in a kind of feverish tremor. Sometimes they would start slowly—almost conversationally—and build to an electrifying conclusion, like the closing statement of a noisy trial attorney. At other times, they would strike like a big fish grabbing a hook and running.

I was by turns inadequate and hopeless, then defiant and courageous. My courage, such as it was, consisted mostly in feigning indifference to the repetitive loop of accusations that seemed determined to grind away at me: You are weak. You are afraid of your own shadow, completely gutless. You are without talent or skill, useless to anyone. You are all talk. You don't care about anyone or anything. You have no integrity, and would sell out in a heartbeat. You are lazy. You will die ignorant and fearful, having understood nothing.

It was stunning that I could be so much more vicious toward myself than toward anyone else, and I had to accept that I didn't know what to do about it. What I did know was that, whatever happened, I was committed to this path of interior observation—mostly because all the alternatives were so full of despair.

7.

In June, when the campus shut down between spring and summer academic quarters, I decided to use what little money I had for a ten day visit first to Burgundy and then the Mosel River Valley, where some of the best German wines are made. This would be a solo trip. Having led students on tours of both the Bordeaux and Burgundy regions by then, I was ready to be free of the tour guide role. Though the campus building in Tours was usually emptied out during the three-week break, the directors had given me a key and agreed to allow me to return early and hole up in my apartment until classes resumed. This was only because I made clear to them that I didn't have the money to travel for the full three weeks.

Going back to Burgundy was a kind of personal pilgrimage, part of the huge contradiction I was living out. I could never deny my enormous respect for the villages strung out along the Cote d'Or, and for the surrounding vineyards that produced the greatest of the world's Pinot Noirs. After all the sitting meditation I had done—what a surprise—I was still a wine geek.

It never even occurred to me to deprive myself during my few days in the town of Beaune. I told myself that if I had to spend relatively lavish amounts of money to enjoy good examples of classic dishes like *jambon persillé* or *coq au vin*, then I would cut short my stay by a day or two. I just needed enough gas money to get back to Tours. This was my idea of budgeting.

What I remember best about that visit, though, was not the food or my visits to winemakers—though I did my best to make those memorable. The most wonderful part came later in the evening, after the delicious dinners I couldn't afford, when I was back in my room, doing my meditation practices, using a bundled up green chenille bedspread as a cushion. It was very odd but: after an hour or so of sitting, though my legs and back were feeling the strain, I began to feel light. Even a little giddy. It was the effects of the anonymity that had felt so liberating back in my apartment. It was wonderful to be in that old hotel in Beaune, France, in 1973, with the distinct feeling that I was not in anyone's mind. There was no family member, no friend, no enemy who was laying out the plot lines of further adventures. I was not being handled by anyone's psyche, wished into some shape I had no interest in assuming. I was convinced I was completely anonymous and unmoored on the earth, and that impression carried delight. Years later, when I had done more reading, I would try to leverage some retroactive self-importance out of the experience by citing the beautiful poem of St. John of The Cross, "Dark Night":

On a dark night, Kindled in love with yearnings—
oh, happy chance!—
I went forth without being observed, my house
being now at rest.

In the happy night, In secret, when none saw me,
Nor I beheld aught, Without light or guide, save
That which burned in my heart.

I couldn't have inflated myself more if I had filled
my colon with helium. The only thing possibly burning in my heart then was the peppercorn sauce on the
duck breast I had at dinner. But that curious anonymity was a genuinely good feeling, and I was grateful
for it.

It was almost by chance that I ended up spending
a night in the little town of Sierck-les-Bains. There
was not much to recommend it, a little town with a
small chateau, a spot along the river about twelve
miles from the German border. I decided to spend the
night because it was where I ended up after a long
day of driving from Beaune.

I had supper in the modest dining room of the
hotel. Though the meal was good, there was nothing remarkable about it; so it was disconcerting that
halfway through I should be overwhelmed with such
a feeling of gratitude for it—the crackling, friendly
bread; the warm richness of the stew; the cool crisp-
ness of the salad greens—that I could feel my composure slipping. For someone who was becoming
pleased with his invisibility, being unnoticed in these

kinds of places, it was alarming. I mean, how would it look to be sitting alone at a table, suddenly weeping uncontrollably?

Ducking into the WC saved me, but still I was disturbed by my loss of composure. Not like me at all, especially in public. After dinner, because it was still sunny and warm, I decided to take my copy of Dietrich Bonhoeffer's *Life Together* and do some reading sitting out on a bench near the *quai*. That spot was a little crowded for my taste, so I walked about a hundred yards upstream, sat down in a tangle of grasses and wildflowers, and started reading. It was a peculiar, unfamiliar kind of well-being that ambushed me then. I just loved being there, with the warm sun and cool breeze, the smell of the grass and wildflowers, the silver ribbon of the river in front of me. A middle-aged woman came strolling by with her little spaniel on a leash, just beside me, on a path where the weeds had been cut. I looked up at her pleasant-looking face. She smiled, so I ventured a "Bonsoir, Madame." She replied, "Bonsoir!" She walked by, then stopped and turned to face me. She broke into a huge grin. "On est bien ici!" she said. "Oui, tres bien," I stammered, swept up by another enormous wave of appreciation, barely able to catch the sob in my throat. I had never before felt sensations at once so powerful and yet so peaceful.

Returning to the Tours campus, I spent the next twelve days alone in the cavernous, dark campus building, going out only for walks and to buy supplies. There was not enough money for more than a couple of café visits, so there was plenty of time for sitting meditation.

Besides providing me the space to observe my thoughts, I realized that solitude also became a way to escape the sort of unintended spell we all tend to cast on each other when we are in groups, doing things that groups of people do, like making money, attracting or repelling each other, talking about the weather or the kids or sports or politics. The unconscious conspiracy we engage in with other people: I'll reinforce your invented world if you'll reinforce mine. We can look each other in the eye and silently agree that the world is like *this*, though of course we know on some level that it's a lie, that we don't have a clue. But it's a useful lie, a comfortable lie, a lie we can live with. Who wants Truth, anyway? I could sense that actual Truth would incinerate me in a second. Is that what I wanted? Of course it was. I remember reading a quote from some mystic or other: "Enough of phrases and conceits and metaphors—I want burning, burning, BURNING!"

I was tinder dry, just waiting for a spark.

8.

I had prepared myself for the reopening of the campus, the circus of noise and activity that was bound to be a shock after nearly two weeks of solitude and silence. What I was not prepared for was the package that appeared just a few days later on the desk in my broom closet of an office. It was from Dan Moynier, the friend who had given me the purple book, who had told me about the job in France. Dan the Trickster.

It was another book, with a note attached to it: "This guy will be speaking in Saanen, Switzerland, in August. You should go. My friend Alan Hooker will be there and you can meet him."

I was looking at a glossy yellow cover featuring a photo of an angular, white-haired, grave-looking man with prominent nose and deep set eyes peering back at me. The title was *Flight of the Eagle*, the author was Jiddu Krishnamurti. Dan had told me about him before, not that I had actually been listening. I remembered nothing other than the fact that Krishnamurti was some sort of Indian philosopher/sage. Dan had also mentioned the name Alan Hooker, who owned a restaurant in Ojai, near Santa Barbara, where Dan had worked as a busboy during his high school years. He had insisted that Alan was the wisest person he knew. I had been just about as interested in his story as I was in Krishnamurti's, but after all, it was Dan who had given me the purple book, so I was sure as hell going to give this new one a try.

I thought I would skim through the first chapter, just to get the feel of it, but gave up on that idea immediately. This book had to be read slowly, a page or two at a time. If other books were watered wine that one could drink almost carelessly, quaffing and gulping, this book was like cognac. It was so dense and concentrated, I was exhausted after three pages. There was a spare quality to it, a diamond-like clarity that demanded the full attention of the reader. I thought of it as a kind of zen book, without that word appearing anywhere in it.

Scanning the table of contents a little later, I was snagged by a chapter heading that had obvious interest for me as a newbie practitioner: "Meditation." I flipped over to the page, and read:

> We are always seeking some form of mystery because we are so dissatisfied with the life we lead, with the shallowness of our activities, which have very little meaning and to which we try to give significance; but this is an intellectual act which therefore remains superficial, tricky, and in the end meaningless.

I took a deep breath, unsure whether I was pleased or horrified that this guy should be reading me more clearly than I was reading him. It was warm and still that night, with sweet, dank riversmell hanging in the moist air, so I walked over to the footpath behind the municipal library, sat down on a bench next to a lamp post, and read more. It was exciting and disturbing to read familiar words used in ways that forced me to recognize their precise meanings, though the whole effect went beyond those meanings. It was paradoxical and then some. Not far from where I had left off was this:

> Has search any meaning at all? Most religious people are always talking about seeking truth; and we are asking if truth can ever be sought after. In the idea of seeking, of finding, is there not also the idea of recognition—the idea that if I find something I must be able to recognize it? Does not recognition imply that I have already known it? Is truth "recognizable"—in the sense of its having already been experienced, so that one is able to say "This is it"? So what is the value of seeking at all? Or, if there is no value in it, is there value only in constant observation, constant listening?—which is not the same as seeking.

I kept trying to take his whole discussion apart, punch some holes in it, *something*. But it was like a brick wall, each word laid carefully upon the others. How long I sat there, how much more I read, all those details are gone now; what remained was stunned recognition, some lightly-scorched brain circuitry that evoked my whole-hearted assent to something that didn't require my or anyone else's assent. It just was.

After reading the book, there was never a doubt that I was going to Switzerland. What was surprising was that there were a few students at the campus who had heard of Krishnamurti and who were enthusiastic about going along. Among them was Greg Wiedeman, a bearded, bear-like fellow with surprisingly gentle manners and great knitting skills; Andy Blasden, an intense, earnest seeker who would tell anyone who would listen about the abuses of his domineering father, a wealthy banker; and Betsy Graeber, a full-tilt, extroverted red-head—articulate, candid, and bonkers. Stories circulated at the campus about her sitting naked on the edge of her bed, hunched over, talking at length about her clitoral responses to various penis types.

There was also Jessup Landry. Jess was a blonde, blue-eyed tomboy from Colorado, who since her arrival at the campus in March had had the courage not just to have coffee with me many times, but—as someone who was already familiar with the purple book—to participate in esoteric discussions that would have put a lesser woman into therapy, or at least a deep sleep state. She was also willing to become involved with me sexually. It happened despite my previous ill-advised sexual encounter, and with full knowledge of all the problems built into a gossip-magnet relationship between a student and an administrative figure, albeit a lowly one.

Though we did our best to make sex as important as our hormones insisted it should be, we never quite managed it. Was it because of our shared, world-class repression—mine issuing from the remains of earnest Catholicism, hers from too many Presbyterian summer camps? Possibly. But also in the mix was a deep bond between two people who passionately acknowledged the importance of the purple book's message, a message that always—sometimes annoyingly and inconvenient-ly—took the priority position in our relationship.

A day before Krishnamurti's talks were to begin, the five of us crammed into my little red Fiat sedan and drove to Switzerland. It was a surreal three days, camp-ing out in the sharp, brilliant mountain air of the little village of Saanen, eating whatever we could afford, usu-ally from the local baker and from a cheese merchant who sold the most amazing apple yogurt.

On the morning of the first talk, we drank hot tea and ate fresh pastries before walking over to the mead-ow where a large white tent had been erected. As it came into view, I was almost in a trance. The alpine sky was a thick, rich blue; the scene around the tent was all green mountains and sweeps of wildflowers. The lower hillsides were dotted with cows whose tinkling bells just served to accentuate the silence that surrounded us. I kept thinking of a particular bit of copy on the back cover of *Flight of the Eagle*. A questioner asks: Sir, what do you want us people here in this world to do? And the beginning of Mr. K's answer is something like: Sir, I don't want anything. That's first. And second: live, live in this world. The world is so marvelously beautiful.

Seated in the tent, I realized how much anticipation I carried with me. I was completely focused on seeing this man, listening to him, absorbing whatever was in the air.

I was intent for very good reasons, all related to the deeply-felt idealism of a young person. Most important among them was my feeling that though I had met a reasonable number of people in my life up to that point—some truly intelligent, entertaining, affectionate, impressive, bigger-than-life people—I had never encountered anyone I was willing to call "wise." Certainly none of the Catholic figures who populated my childhood. The word "wise" implied qualities that went beyond simply being smart or successful, or even thoughtful or inspirational. I was willing to attach that word only to those who seemed to me to have been able to plunge into the deepest paradoxes involved in being alive; not just through thoughts and words, but actually somehow living the reality of those mysteries. Were these people *saints*? I wasn't about to weigh in on that one. I knew only that there was a precious thread of this insane behavior running through our known history and probably preceding it: people sitting for years in desert caves or high up in rugged mountain ranges, others wandering as mendicants or creating physical exercises to hone the powers of perception. I saw these crazy people as the only ones I could ever trust and respect.

I was anxious, feeling that I might be about to encounter one of them.

I closed my eyes, focused my breath on the tip of my nose. There was little crowd murmur, considering the size of a group that must have numbered three or four hundred. Then he appeared, walking up the center aisle, an absurdly small person in a pair of dress slacks, white shirt and beige cardigan sweater. After getting some help arranging the microphone around his neck, he peered out at the crowd as the buzz died out. He spoke in a posh, English public school accent that enveloped his reedy, tenor-ish voice.

"I wonder," he said, "I wonder what all of you are doing here?"

A nervous chuckle from the audience.

"Are you here to enjoy an entertainment, a diversion from your everyday life? Or perhaps you are here to have an outing, a pleasant sojourn in these beautiful surroundings—the meadows, the hills, the fresh air. Have you come perhaps hoping to hear something from the speaker that will solve your problems, some idea that will make sense of all the confusion, the misery, the conflict in the life of each one of us?"

The silence in the interval between his sentences seemed lush and rich; the microphone was so sensitive that the sound of his lips parting before he spoke was like being physically touched. For that hour and a half I was as focused as I had ever been in my life, and I had to admit it was because I was one of those who wanted answers. I knew there weren't any, but I suppose I had to demonstrate that I was serious about the search. I told myself in those first few minutes of the talk: if you are ever going to pay complete attention to *anything*, this is the moment to do it. Yet I just kept bumping into myself everywhere I turned; it wasn't lost on me that my own inner jabbering would keep me from really hearing this guy I had come such a long way to hear.

The thing that finally awed me into silence and at the same time set me on fire was not any specific thing he said. It was more the realization that this was a person who had completely given himself over to this work, who had decided to spend his life exploring the most impenetrable issues confronting human beings, the ones most of us pass over because they seem too obscure, or because we get caught up in something more immediate, or because we look around and don't see anyone else doing it. Not only was this man unafraid; he seemed to revel in the task.

When the talk ended, I walked out of the tent, took fifteen or twenty steps into the tall grass, laid down, and fell asleep.

9.

After the talk the following day, I decided to find the guesthouse where Dan Moynier's friends, Alan and Helen Hooker, were staying. The others wanted to come along, so we trooped off down the main street of Saanen. It turned out to be an easy find in such a small town, and within fifteen minutes we were being led into the living room of a trim little chalet to meet Alan. As I walked in I could feel myself withdrawing into a skeptical little cocoon. Who was this guy anyway? My friend Dan always talked him up, saying Alan was a "teacher" and a "sage." I thought: How big a deal can he be? He owns a restaurant, he's a vegetarian and a psychic. Great. So what?

When I saw Alan, sitting in a rocking chair, he seemed like a pleasant old guy in his nice brown wool slacks and red plaid shirt, buttoned up to the neck. He was a fairly big man, over six feet, with a pretty serious stomach on him. His hair was pure white and thin, his smile warm, his eyes penetrating, with a dose of troublemaker in them. I had no idea when I shook hands with him that he was to be perhaps my greatest friend, one who would in many ways be a father to me, who would save my life.

We were all a little nervous, possibly because we were suddenly seated in an immaculately clean, tastefully decorated living room, and couldn't help realizing that we were seriously scruffy—aromatic even. We were served tea in beautiful bone china cups. After I recounted our all-night drive and current status at the campground, there was a silence that no one seemed willing to fill. Jessie finally broke the silence.

"I have to say, I don't want to do an autopsy on what we heard over there. It seems better to just leave it alone."

Alan observed that that was a perfectly reasonable response to such an intense experience. He said we are frequently so full of noise from outside that K's talks provoke a kind of interior "brush-clearing" that creates space for silence. But, he said, the talks can also create urgent and intense discussion. "There is no 'correct' response," he said.

Betsy said, "The thing I have a hard time getting past is that he's an Indian man, with a certain upbringing—I know he's a Brahmin and doesn't smoke or drink or eat meat. So how can we, a bunch of American students, get to the spiritual places where he lives every day?"

I noticed that Alan did not jump right in, but looked down and allowed a few moments of silence before saying, "It's doubtful anyone could inhabit the places where Mr. K lives, if we are going to phrase it that way, and it would almost certainly not be appropriate for them to try. His aim is not to have us emulate him, but to throw responsibility for our awareness right back on us."

We peppered him with questions then, picking up momentum, getting excited about the discussion (which translated to talking loudly and verbally steamrolling one another). Alan smiled and raised a hand. "One thing you might consider is that the answer to your question is very often right in the question itself. I don't mean that in some symbolic way, but literally. When you ask a question, consider the words, the concepts you're using. The framework of ideas you grab hold of will tell you a lot about what you want to hear—or don't want to hear. A lot about your desires in asking the question. The words you choose are full of clues about the conclusions you've made, the ones that underpin your whole way of looking at the world. Try it for a little while. It can be very useful." After a pause, he said, "To go a bit deeper, consider that it is rarely our conscious conclusions that hold sway and wreak havoc in our lives; it is almost always the unconscious, unobserved ones that run the show. It is intriguing to ask why more of us don't take the time to find out what they are. I have often considered that question."

Andy spoke up: "And do you find the answer in *your* question?" His smile was challenging.

"An-dyyy!" Jessie looked a little annoyed.

Alan burst out with a belly laugh. "Oh, my God, yes! You see, I am an iconoclastic type, which means I am interested in power...but from the point of view of the disempowered." More laughter. "When I was a boy, I was very stubborn and independent. No one was going to tell me what to do! So it is not surprising to hear me use phrases like "hold sway" and "running the show." That's power language. But even these kinds of observation just scratch the surface. The real heart of exploration is wordless. It isn't a mental commitment, it's a passion. If you have that passion, you do it. If not—then some other time. But in any case you will find out for yourself. You wouldn't want anyone spoiling your adventure for you."

I had to speak up. "So what do you believe?"

Alan smiled at me for a long moment. "If by that you mean some creed—or doctrine—that I use to describe life, its meaning, and such: I don't have any. I am content to watch, to observe, to find out. What is interesting to me is that I find I have an enormous amount of faith. Not faith in anyone or anything, mind you. Just enormous faith."

After Switzerland, I worked at the campus for another eight weeks. I was strangely quiet inside about my imminent return to California. I had a job lined up in a wine and liquor store in San Carlos, a larger, more swank operation than the one I had left to come to France. It was a plan that seemed to me the perfect level of commitment to money-making and physical survival, but one which scandalized Jessie with its lack of ambition. "Are you really going to go back and work in another liquor store?" she asked. My answer was, "And this, from a third-year Art History major?"

It was clearer than ever that my life was to be about the interior landscape, the confrontation with the self that the purple book called Tapasia, the test, the fire. It eclipsed everything else, finally: geography, money, people—even romantic partners. I had to get to the bottom of these odd, resonant sayings that were thick on the ground in the purple book and in *Flight of the Eagle*.

Somewhere in my outraged, bruised, obsessive, idealistic mind, this was the truth. I would never have talked about it, though, either because I was too afraid of it or because none of it was easily expressed. As soon as I made the attempt, with Jessie or anyone else, it sounded like bad motivational speaking, or a set piece read by a salesman. Out in front of me there stretched a blank, a nothing, an everything—something I was desperate for, and something I knew nothing about. It wasn't art. It wasn't science. It would make a terrible pick-up line and a worse resumé item, but it was burning inside me as my heart's desire.

10.

Back in California, I stayed with Dan Moynier and blitzed through an intense apartment hunt. Was it just me, or was the 1973 economy completely in the toilet? People in cars and on the streets seemed haggard, stressed, slack-jawed. I looked at cramped in-law apartments and flimsy modern one-bedrooms with cottage cheese ceilings and globes hanging on bronze chains in the bathrooms. I looked in Redwood City, Palo Alto, Los Altos—at that time all more or less accessible even to low wage workers like me, and not yet places where home ownership goes to die.

At the end of the first week, I saw an ad for a place in Woodside. Like everything in that exclusive community, it was expensive—$200 a month—but the ad had the words "peaceful" and "redwoods" in it. I sped up into the hills and rented it on the spot. A two-story in-law apartment, the lower part was older and darker, with a low ceiling that made the kitchenette and living space seem even smaller. But then there was the upstairs, whose newer design and construction looked like heaven to me. A light and airy bedroom with a small, tidy bath attached. Eggshell walls, open beam ceiling, wood-framed gothic windows, rust-colored shag carpet that made a luxurious bed compared to the thin carpet remnant I became used to in France. And there was the view. Infused with a rich, filtered green light, the scene was of huge, graceful redwoods, various ferns and groundcover, and a few hulking, burnt-out stumps looking like carefully placed sculpture.

I loved the way sounds were milky and muted there. It made the silence even richer, reminding me of the quality of the air in the tent in Saanen moments before Mr. K would begin speaking.

I had never lived anywhere with a night-sky bonus, either. The stars at night were like tiny, brilliant shards of something precious. I would sometimes walk outside, look up and find one star among the thousands, usually a more faint and shy one rather than a brassy bright attention-getter. I would focus on it, staring hard, ignoring everything else until all the other stars disappeared through some optical illusion. I felt my thoughts scattering, like insects shooed away. It seemed like my star's light was racing to reach my eyes, though I knew it had been traveling its impersonal path for hundreds or even thousands of years. I wanted to send the light from my eyes out to meet it.

Then there was my job. Though I myself was quite clear about the role that Brannigan's Wines and Spirits would play in providing money to support my explorations, old acquaintances and my parents saw it very differently. In their alternate version of the narrative, I was collecting myself, preparing to jump onto a fast track to something or other. After my little European *divertissement*, I was going to buckle down and do something important. Make something of myself.

Jessie had returned to her studies at Mills College, in Oakland, and I was seeing her on many of my days off. It was downright strange that with sex still such a low-priority we should be so easy around each other. Or maybe it wasn't strange at all: sex can be an explosive device in more ways than one. As it was, there was delight and tolerance; and though the latter could as easily have been rooted in repression as in consideration, it worked. She touched me with her honest, tomboy attitudes. I could make her laugh.

She continued to insist—often enough to be annoying—that I should go back to school. But my job at Brannigan's had a major advantage over any more ambitious path: I could leave it behind every day. I didn't have to care about it. Professional training was out of the question because it would force me to identify with the work, take it home, stew in it, think about it when I woke from sleep in the night's silence. I was not willing to do that.

I didn't see myself as a miscreant loner or some kind of Junior Ascetic, but it was clear to me that my only real job was to climb down into myself and explore all the spooky caverns, all the booby traps and tripwires and funhouse features lodged down deep where I had never looked. I saw that being in Woodside was not basically much different from being in France. It was all adventure, all a series of potential discoveries. Like the purple book said: When you know how to listen, everyone is your teacher. So all I needed was a quiet place to live, a little money to manage physical survival, and the time to learn about myself.

I can't precisely conjure up my mindset during the year I worked at the store, if only because it meant so little to me. Most often my survival strategy was to stay out of everyone's way and stick to my job description, which was to stock the wine shelves, give customer recommendations, keep the warehouse neat, and pitch in at the registers.

I hadn't counted on the sensory overload aspect of the work. It brought into sharp focus a realization that had been rattling around in my head since before going to France, which was that I was a total naïf, and that the more shocking, ugly scenarios in the normal life of commerce would always leave me dumbfounded and unable to respond, viz., the salesman who brought in a few samples of the great 1971 white Burgundies, gave us a taste, then whispered laughingly: "Goes great with pussy!" Having been in Europe doing what I was doing, I had forgotten much of this. Brannigan's refreshed my memory.

Predictably, my self-criticism machine went into vicious-cycle overdrive. Was I just dying to disapprove of the people I was encountering, itching to beat them over the head with what I knew, like some budding tent-revival zealot, repeating the wisdom until it completely lost its octane rating and became some kind of verbal elevator music? Did I want to separate myself from the rest of humanity and be alone at last with my splendid understanding? Was this what I wanted? My internal noise only served to make me more determined than ever to explore and then explore some more.

There was no television, no radio in my apartment; not even the limited amount of music I had had in my place in France. This was unnerving at first, and though I told myself I should buy a sound system or a television, I never did. After a few months I began to feel at home with silence. It felt positively un-American.

I read the New Testament aloud, a bit at a time, nearly every evening. I read it as if I had never seen it before, like it was a strange bit of anthropology that needed studying. I read the Koran after that, also aloud. That was real *terra incognita*. I thought: This is a work that has inspired millions of people over many centuries. There must be *something* in it, so I should give it a hearing. I read every word of it, slowly, giving the phrases inflection and meaning even when the ideas seemed banal, or when I was mired in one of the long stretches of text that were stultifyingly repetitive. I put myself in front of the Koran the way I had put myself in front of the paintings in the Prado or the Louvre, the way I had listened to Krishnamurti in Switzerland: If there was something of value there, I wanted to receive it, even without consciously knowing it. *Preferably* without consciously knowing it.

I practiced meditation twice a day now, in the very early morning and just before bed. I was still about as limber as a tongue depressor, and after an hour or so of focusing on my breath and watching the mad parade of my thoughts, my legs and back, as they always had, complained enough to have me leave off. The way I now explained to myself my willingness to endure the strain of all this sitting was: At the end of the day, when confusion from the torrent of events—the million-and-one stimuli and the noises in my head—threatened to over-whelm and bury me, sitting was a refuge. It was a place I could point to and say: At the very least, when nothing is known or understood, when it's all dismal gibberish and the blur of living is a noisy emptiness without an ounce of heart or validity, I can sit down right on *that* particular spot on the floor, right *there*…and watch.

Something else kept coming back to me, too, as it had in France. Most of the pain I felt didn't come from any effort I might have put into sitting still. It's just not that hard to do. Most of it came from the resistance of my muscles. Whatever force kept them clenched tight did not want to be sitting there quietly. It wanted to zoom ahead to the next thing, and the next. To dinner, or a walk, or whatever. Or just as often it was stuck in the past, with some obsession that had upset or delighted it. Putting myself in this particular physical position taught me that the issue is binary and simple. Either I'm "here," or I'm not anywhere. I couldn't be in the past or in the future, for reasons that are pretty straightforward and temporal. If on top of that I was going to resist being "here," then I was the one responsible for preventing myself from truly, wholly being anywhere. This was, after all, the bedrock meaning of the purple book's title, *Be Here Now*.

I was more than dimly aware that my image of the world might appear pretty nutty to some. Why would a twenty-four year-old man living in California in 1974 hold tight to this stuff? He should be out at bars, kick-ing the tires, trying to find a mate. He should be start-ing a career, getting life insurance, buying a set of stur-dy cookware, subscribing to *Consumer Reports*. But whenever I started to flog myself for being so odd, it just served to flip a switch on another tape loop, one that said: No point in getting too critical. After all, who are these people who are describing to you what your life should be? Are they great admirable personages to whom I instinctively pay respect? Not really. They are more like the same poor slob I am, but with maybe an even slightly keener sense of conformity. Who knows, maybe even a clearer instinct for grounded, solid life choices. But whatever the society around me had to offer was not so devastatingly beautiful that I had to spend time feeling bad about not hurling myself to the ground, prostrate at its feet.

That December, as Christmas approached, Jessie headed back to Colorado and my growing desire to be alone prodded me to beg off spending the holidays with my parents. As a junior member of the staff at the store, I was scheduled to work both Christmas Eve and Christmas Day. I wasn't happy about it. After my resentful shift on the 24th, I told myself I needed to do something special for my solo Christmas dinner, but the only store I could find open was a nearby Safeway. As I wandered the aisles under the buzzy-bright fluorescents, I began an internal dialogue about the appropriateness of a "fancy" dinner for Christmas. Was it a meaningless indulgence, an excuse to engage in personal greed? I stood in front of the meat section for a minute, wound up and ready to snap. Buy the wrong item and you fail. I postponed the painful moment by heading over to the produce section and bagging up some broccoli. Broccoli was a safe purchase because I wasn't that fond of it.

Finally, I came back to meat and poultry, trying to look casual as I scanned the smooth, bulgy, plastic-wrapped trays of steaks, chops and chicken. I lusted after a pack that held one thick T-bone steak whose red color looked almost fluorescent itself. With a glass of Cabernet, this would be a feast fit for…what? Christmas? What did a T-bone steak have to do with it? In a sudden jerky movement, I grabbed a pack of two half-breasts of chicken and bolted for the check stand.

On Christmas Day, the store closed at six and I was home by seven. I had brought home a bottle of Sonoma County Chardonnay, and after I changed clothes I got busy fixing my holiday dinner. I refused to notice my nervousness, my disapproval of what I was doing. I put the chicken breasts into my lone Pyrex baking dish, sprinkled them with chopped garlic, salt and pepper, and a few shakes of a jar of Italian herbs I had bought, then poured some of the wine over it. My hands shook as I pushed the dish into the oven. Then I sat down to read.

I was in the middle of The Bhagavad Gita, the ancient Sanskrit poem I had often read in France. Though I was not especially attracted to Hinduism's pantheon of various animal gods—monkeys and elephants, whatever—I had to admit that this slim volume scored major points for simplicity and beauty.

I read for a while, aloud, just as I had done with the Koran and the New Testament, until my dinner pried my attention away. It smelled disturbingly wonderful. Good enough that I began to regret having cooked it. I thought of Nikos Kazantzakis's book on the life of Saint Francis. In it, there was a moment when Francis tastes his soup, and is so alarmed by its delicious flavor that he immediately reaches into the ashes at the edge of the hearth and throws a handful into his bowl.

I took the dish out of the oven for a moment, the steamy perfume filling my nostrils. I pushed and prodded it with a fork, then put it back. I turned on the burner under a pot of broccoli florets. I read more, but could feel the interior conflict getting in the way. I read:

> Set thou, therefore, thy senses in harmony,
> and then slay thou sinful desire,
> the destroyer of vision and wisdom.

This was disturbing, especially because I had been training myself to pay close attention to whatever scripture I was reading, to take it seriously. With the Koran, infusing the verses with meaning was a tough slog; the Bhagavad Gita, on the other hand, went right for the throat.

I got up, pulled the dish out of the oven and put it on the stovetop. I turned off the broccoli. The chicken was brown at the edges, sizzling. Rivulets of fat floated on the cooking liquid. I was hungry. I speared one of the chicken breasts and put it on a plate with the broccoli, then poured myself a glass of the Chardonnay and sat down at my tiny table, two steps from the stove. My book sat open, spine upwards, as I took my first bite. Surprised at how good it tasted, I wolfed down a few more bites before returning to my book. I cut some bite-sized pieces to allow me to hold the book in my left hand and still eat with the fork in my right. I hunched over my plate, wanting less distance between the chicken and my mouth.

In the story, the god Krishna was working up some momentum in telling the king, Arjuna, about the importance of yoga and its relationship to right action. I was doing a lot more eating than reading when I came to this:

> Kill therefore with the sword of wisdom the doubt
> born of ignorance that lies in thy heart.
> Be one in self-harmony, in Yoga,
> and arise, great warrior, arise.

Who knows why certain passages of books affect one person strongly and another not at all? Or why some will strike you powerfully at one moment, though you might pass right by them at another? I read that last line, and my voice broke. Before I could put down my book—or my fork, for that matter—I was sobbing uncontrollably. I did not try to stop myself, as I normally would have. When the sobs tapered off, I wiped my face with my paper napkin and continued reading. I made no attempt to explain any of it to myself.

11.

Other than time spent with Jessie, I had close to no social life. The year in France loosened whatever bonds I had had with people previously, and I made no effort to renew them. Dan Moynier had moved to Santa Barbara to take a job doing PR for a restaurant chain, and, with the exception of an occasional anxious phone call, my parents were eerily silent.

When my work shifts ended, if I didn't stop to buy supplies, I drove straight home. Often my mind would rage, demanding I stop for a beer or a glass of wine at a café, or to see a movie. I kept my eyes on the road, determined not to act on the thoughts, ferocious as they were. I focused on deep breathing as my car made its way up the winding road into the darkness of the hills.

My solitude in Woodside was much more complete than the one I experienced at the campus in France; it was more like the magical moment in Burgundy when I seemed to slip the tether of other peoples' expectations and attention. The only expectations of me now were those few that rested on an easily replaceable store clerk who dropped off the planet when he punched out on the time clock.

Once I reached home, the urge to be somewhere else dropped away. I wasn't at all starved for company. Beyond morning and evening meditations, my free time was spent reading, going for walks, or sitting on a kitchen chair outside my front door, breathing the redwood-infused air. The depth of the silence was overwhelming: a palpable, untamed presence that I learned to be attentive to. I respected it. It was so high I couldn't get over it, so low I couldn't get under it.

Life changed in January of 1974, when I made three friends. Looking back, I think I was working in the shop just in order to meet George and Miles and Dinah. They were roughly my age, living in San Carlos as caretakers of the 6-acre estate of George and Dinah's great uncle. It was an idyllic life, lived in a beautiful bungalow surrounded by an array of trees and flowering plants that made the property a botanical showcase. They spent their time caring for these, and keeping a seasonal garden that provided a constant supply of spectacular vegetables for their great uncle and themselves.

George and Miles were inseparable friends who had worked together in a landscaping business, while Dinah—George's sister and Miles's fiancée—had left her job as a Pan-Am flight attendant, happy to keep house and do much of the cooking. The first time I saw their home, with its tastefully simple furnishings, its bright, buoyant feel, and its spectacular collection of coleus plants, it made me a little giddy with recognition. These were my people.

We met in the shop one rainy afternoon when they

came looking for new wines to try. George took the lead, with booming voice and big gestures. His personality matched his height and his dramatic Abraham Lincoln facial features. Miles was quiet, intense, and built on a much smaller scale, with fair hair and a wry smile. His sly injections of humor seasoned George's talkative bursts. ("Make sure to sell George something expensive enough that he won't drink it all in ten minutes.") Dinah was a sweet dynamo of a woman with a fluty, musical voice, huge gray eyes, and a crooked-tooth smile. Her sunny manner didn't prevent her from firmly herding the boys when she felt they needed it.

My wine recommendations over a period of weeks led to a dinner invitation. I agreed to come, but was conflicted. Of course. My hermetic side objected sternly, insisting that social events like this were just distractions from the inner work. So I was going to the home of these people I barely knew, to fill my stomach and get drunk?

I knew I had made the right decision the moment I arrived. I felt warmed and welcomed by these people, whose eyes were full of a sweet energy and openness that tempered the arid discipline I had been pursuing. I brought a couple of solid but modest wines, something I got in the habit of doing each time I went to visit, and all three of them pitched in to cook a great meal. They, along with much of America at that time, were devouring (so to speak) Julia Child's book, *The French Chef*, experimenting with the most complicated recipes ("A handful at a time, twist the minced mushrooms in the corner of a kitchen towel..."), and that first night we ate Veal Prince Orloff. Or something close to it. It was a digestion-stopping, artery-bursting tour de force that, if a little on the gloppy side, tasted wonderful with the Bordeaux I had brought along.

In response to their gentle curiosity about me, I initially stuck to the most colorful stories of my year in France rather than telling them about the heart of my life. It was a little like talking about the popcorn you ate and not the movie you saw, but I reasoned that there was no point in trying to explain something so personal, something that I couldn't explain well even to myself. I needn't have worried. All three turned out to be burnt-out Catholics who, without having run the gauntlet of Catholic schools, had seen enough of catechism class to share my issues with organized religion. This gave me an opening to talk, very generally at first, about the revelations that had changed the world for me. Their combination of skepticism and open-mindedness allowed for many wonderful discussions about the meaning of meditation and the value of silence and introspection—but there were, of course, many more about wine and food.

At home late after that first dinner, I might well have tortured over being caught in the crosshairs of pleasure, but there was something so heartfelt about the three of them and our evening together that I had to let it go. As I laid down on the floor wrapped in my blanket, I felt myself relax, trusting in the flow of these events and the rightness of a budding friendship.

On the phone, I told Jessie all about George, Miles, and Dinah, and that I had volunteered her to have dinner with them on her next visit. I was a little worried about it. You want people that you like to like each other. I

later joked that what I should have been worried about
was that she and Dinah would get along so well that
we males would feel a little neglected. Over another
Herculean—or rather Dionysian—cooking effort, called
coulibiac of salmon *en croute* (salmon, mushrooms,
and wild rice in a pastry crust, with mock hollandaise,
if you're keeping score), there was more bonding. Jess
and I signed on to help that spring and summer with the
garden the trio was about to plant on nearly a tenth of an
acre. It turned out to be such a success that, as it grew,
George voiced the concern of all of us: Sweet Jesus,
who was going to eat all this *food*?

Through the spring, Jess came down nearly every
weekend, even on days I was working. In the mornings,
she would leave me alone to do my yoga and my sitting, and walk up to the little store at Skylonda to buy a
newspaper. Sometimes we were quiet around each other
for long periods; sometimes she would tell me more
about her life, her classes, the other young women in
her dorm. She often talked about feeling like an idiot
getting a degree in Art History. I told her I didn't see
any reason to worry too much about how you earn your
money. Hey, I was working in a liquor store. I know
you are, she would say, rolling her eyes and shaking her
head. You shouldn't be in that place, and you know it,
etc. I laughed and told her she sounded like my mother.
We talked about the purple book and Krishnamurti,
too. Sometimes she would stop and look at me with a
quizzical smile. "Who are you?" she would ask. My answer—from the purple book, always the same—became
like a punch line. I used it because it was much better

than anything I could ever conjure up, and—okay, the first time—maybe to impress her. I would say, "Just a pattern of energy." She would shake her head and smack me on the arm, saying something like, "You are *such* a terrible bullshitter."

12.

I suggested that Jess move in with me for the summer. It would be a huge change for the fierce loner I had become, but at the same time a safe one. Nothing too open-ended, nothing suggesting permanence. In August she would go back to school for her last year, and I… would do whatever I was going to do. She seemed happy with the idea, and easily found work for the summer organizing youth activities for the Redwood City Parks and Recreation Department. She felt the Woodside apartment was just too small and remote, so I agreed to look for another place. Giving up the little apartment was hard for me, but I said nothing.

It was a short search. In a phone conversation the next day, George told me he knew of just the thing: an old two-bedroom house owned by Jolene and Barney Metzner, a great aunt and uncle of his and Dinah's. It was located in the hills above Redwood City, its major asset being a spectacular view of the bay. The Metzners agreed to rent it for $200 a month, too, which was a sweetheart price. The perfect deal.

After meeting Jolene, a fragile woman in her mid-seventies, with the high cheekbones and incongruously flaming red hair of a faded beauty, I realized that she was as straight-laced as she was sweet. Lots of Norman Vincent Peale in her conversation. This worried me. The Metzner's own home was on the property, and it was hard to imagine her as the willing accomplice of a young couple wanting to live in sin. Why I immediately framed the issue that way had to do with the social mores of the mid-seventies, yes, but even more with the residue of my noxious early Catholic education. On a deep level, my disapproval was a given, but the real question was: could we risk Jolene's? How to be rock-solid certain about getting the house? As if it were the most natural thing in the world, I suggested to Jessie that we masquerade as an engaged couple. Which, well, we might be. Possibly. Sometime.

Jess agreed, having seen the house and gotten as excited about it as I was. So we set up a meeting with Jolene, borrowed a plausible engagement ring from one of Jess's friends, and brazened it out.

We were a hit. Jolene loved Jess, and seemed to experience a vicarious lift from young love—even the misrepresented variety. She told us we could move in at the end of April; I would live there alone until Jess finished school. Jess and I congratulated ourselves all the way back to my place, but after she left I felt a nagging uneasiness. I tried talking sense into myself. These qualms were ridiculous—not to mention inconvenient. Get a hold of yourself. This little lie isn't hurting anyone, and Jess and I will take good care of the house. That's what counts. Jolene would probably have rented the house to us even if she knew we weren't getting married.

In the early evening I sat down cross-legged on my cushion to do my practices. Immediately, I burst into a fit of sobbing. It was annoying, actually, because I felt like such a wimp, but even more because it was going to blow the deal on the house. But I knew exactly what I had to do. I called Jolene, telling her I needed to visit.

"When would you like to come?" she asked, in her slow, quavering, sweet voice.

"Right now, if it's alright with you."

By the time I arrived, I was a little calmer. The whole issue was clear. I explained that Jessie and I were not engaged. Only our fear of losing the little house had made us deceive her. Being especially poor at confrontations, I had to steady my voice many times. Jolene sat completely still as she listened, her face impassive.

"Whether we move into the house or not is beside the point, I realize now," I told her. "The only thing that matters is that I get this whole thing straight with you. That you know the truth. The rest is worthless."

The silence in her living room was pretty thick.

"Well," she said softly, smiling almost imperceptibly, "it must have taken a lot of courage for you to do this. A lot of grace is working through you today." She looked straight into my eyes. "You both seem like fine young people, and…I don't see why we shouldn't rent the little house to you and Jessie anyway." She paused, and smiled more broadly. "That is her real name, isn't it?" And she laughed.

The purple book was right again. Driving home I remembered the line that said, "There's no doubt about it—the truth gets you high." I felt very light and peaceful.

In early May, not quite a month ahead of Jess's arrival, I moved into that little house, with its un-insulated brown walls, threadbare flesh-colored carpet, white enamel kitchen cupboards, and extraordinary view. I realize as I try to zero in on all the events that took place there during the ten months that followed, I will inevitably be tossing out a string of red herrings. Not knowing how to touch the heart of this mysterious time, I will have to settle for handling its flesh and bones, and trust that the bits that are harder to touch will come through.

Through the summer, I spent many hours at the estate where my friends lived, with Jess pitching in when she could. Much of the work was in the vegetable garden, doing things that all my formal education had neglected to teach: thinning carrots, corn and beets; building up mounds for melons; trellising beans. I also helped dig a six-foot-deep compost pit, which involved hours of stripped-to-the-waist, teeth-jarring pickax work, slamming into clay so dense that it yielded only an inch at a time. It was a perfect task for this sporadically ferocious person, the son of my father. I held nothing back, putting every ounce of myself into each stroke of the pick. Yet even through all the strain, I could feel a strange magic in that work, too. Something of me went into the ground, and the ground yielded up something of itself to me. Until that time, I don't believe my thoroughly cerebral self had ever really encountered the earth. The word "mystical" came into my mind. "*This*, I said to myself, "is yoga."

Sometimes after a swim in the late afternoon, I began to feel so good that it seemed out of proportion to the activity I was engaged in. Watering flower beds, I watched the water shoot crystalline from the hose, the air cool with the mineral smell of wet ground all around me. I felt like I *was* that water, spilling life and freshness on everything. The next moment I became the plants, drinking in all the nourishment, the lush bath of water alive.

With Jess moving in at the beginning of June, my life changed radically; but I still carried on my morning and evening sitting meditations. I began experimenting with *pranayam*, or the yoga of breath. The purple book explained how to inhale through the right nostril and out through the left, then the reverse, then in through both and out through both. At first, a few minutes of this left me light–headed from what I figured to be hyperventilation. After a couple of weeks I was doing twenty repetitions and feeling refreshed and calm.

During the warmest weather our pleasure curriculum included splurges on German wines, cold and crisp and light, with names I had worked hard to remember— Rudesheimer Bishofsberg, Graacher Himmelreich, Wehlener Sonnenuhr. We sat out on the little porch in back of the house and smelled the warm asphalt of the school playground across the road, the earthiness of the brush that grew thick on the empty lots scattered across the hill in back of us.

Even while enjoying Jess's company, my affection was more and more tainted with sadness. I could hardly escape admitting that I was too single-mindedly devoted to the discoveries that had set fire to me to allow anything else—or anyone else—to take priority. Whether this was an unquenchable thirst for truth or a deepening manifestation of my berserker nature is a question that will never have a definitive answer. It was a lonely realization, though, one that I never discussed with Jessie. I did not search for a word to describe the deadly earnestness with which, more and more, I approached everything; but if I had, it would probably have been "dedication." Only much later did I see that the word could just as easily have been "ambition." Or even "compulsion."

After about a month together in the house, I could sense, too, that Jess was bored. It was hard to blame her, living with someone who had less and less interest in the world outside, content with an almost monastic lifestyle. Though unspoken, it was clear to both of us that her interest in the purple book and in Krishnamurti did not look like mine. It was not the headlong commitment of a berserker. My zeal might have been attractive to her in some ways, but living with it every day? That was a different story.

One afternoon, when I expressed no interest in going to see the movie *Chinatown*, which had just been released, she began to cry. When I reached for her, putting my hand on her arm, she burst out, "You don't care about me and what I want at all!" How to explain to her? It wasn't that I didn't care about her. It was more that I was already spoken for. On some level, the vows had already been recited.

During that summer, I sometimes felt unaccountably good following meditations: energized and light. It was odd to feel such a quiet but deep sense of well-being, mostly because it was different from anything I had known before. Though not consistent or predictable, it was a feeling that validated everything I was doing, gradually displacing the residue of my hangdog self.

There were also vaguely freakish developments, small changes that in spite of our joking about them invited speculation and inflated significance. One of these was Jess remarking one day that I had begun to smell really good. How not to make a punch line out of that? Yet after all the jokes about how bad I must have smelled before, or about my new cosmic deodorant, or about buying a lifetime supply of the amazing new soap I was using, neither of us could explain the light, fresh, sweet smell that surrounded me then.

The other change was that I always knew the time of day, with a precision that was spooky. We realized this one morning when Jess and I were in the living room, where there were no clocks, and she asked me the time. Unthinking, and without looking at my watch, I told her. We laughed. That was the launch of a parlor game that went on for weeks, until there was no more suspense in it. Lying in bed, walking on the street, reading in the evening, she would suddenly cover my eyes with her hands or grab my wrist to cover my watch and demand I tell her the time. We would laugh hysterically. What other response was there?

Many nights just before sleep, I felt I had already begun dreaming. I would get into bed with her and read a few pages from the purple book, or from some scripture, while she read Kurt Vonnegut novels. After ten or fifteen minutes we tacitly agreed it was time to sleep; there was a calm in the air that was nourishing. I remember looking at her one night just before we turned out the lights, and saying, in a way that was so unbidden it surprised both of us: "I feel like I'm going off on an adventure."

My dreams were usually indistinct, nothing remaining when I woke except a feeling of having taken on a task and completed it handily. As if I had exerted myself and come away fulfilled.

Occasionally they were vivid. One I remember in particular:

It was night, and I was making my way alone through an old, ramshackle house. The furnishings were dusty; the rooms had a stale smell. I made my way upstairs to a second floor, then a third. There were garret bedrooms here, one of which had a window that led me out onto the slate shingle roof. I crawled up to the peak, and my hands grew larger. I began to levitate, experimenting with that feeling as I held onto the peak of the roof's steep pitch. I could see a couple of chimneys and, quite close to me, an old bronze rooster weathervane. I felt myself rise gently above the shingles, hover there for a moment, then come back down. Without thinking, I gave myself a sudden push away from the roof. I felt a sharp jolt of terror as the roof receded and I realized I couldn't get back. I heard myself say, "Oh shiiiiiiit!" What I had done was irrevocable. My heart pounded as momentum carried me slowly away from the roof, into the night sky. If only I had held on, just pinching the tip of the weathervane's arrow between my thumb and index finger, I might have had my levitations yet stayed anchored to the building. Drifting out among the stars, I quickly forgot my fear and frustration. On waking, I felt buoyant, serene, surrounded by a familiar profound silence.

I continually had to ignore the urge to evaluate my practices. I wanted to take my temperature in some way, to measure what was happening, but it was all just a lot of thinking. Was I making "progress"? It was none of my business. I was required only to keep the vigil. The purple book was clear about this. "Am I going backwards or forwards?" it asked. On this journey, there was no location to map and measure. You had to be lost to get anywhere. The book said: Awakening is not a prize or an achievement or a destination. It is a transformation of consciousness.

13.

Jess left in early August to go back up to Mills College. Before she left, we had put on our mature faces and talked seriously about the need for her to finish school, shoring up the logic of that conclusion. We held each other and agreed that if we were going to be together, it could wait until the coming school year was done. I was horribly conflicted about this exchange. Only much later could I finally see that it was a fig leaf that allowed me to hedge my position, to be in her life a little longer. It might well have been more honest to make a clean break with her then, the kind that is abrupt and painful but less ruinous than the excruciating, drawn-out variety. But I wasn't, and I didn't. To put it brutally, I was using her in a subtle way. As I began to sense the power of the solitude that her departure from my life would bring down on my head, I wanted to delay the moment when I would face it directly. I was full of foreboding. And rightly so.

I began to eat less, avoiding meat completely.

Fasting wasn't anything new at that point, of course; the purple book had been very clear in advocating it as one element of self-discipline, the development of the will that would prepare the ground for greater interior exploration. But at its heart, my fasting was a desperation response. The commercial world had exhausted me with its relentless assaults, and academia looked just as bad or possibly worse because of its self-congratulatory veneer of respectability and superiority. The world looked like a crazed, out-of-control orgy of acquisition: work more, own more, control more, and—of course—eat and drink more. In the face of all that, I could hear the purple book loud and clear, telling me that I could be absolutely gorging on all that stimulation and it *still wouldn't be enough*. I could feel the truth of it. I could feel the despair of it. And even now I don't see my fasting response as completely mad. It was extreme in a way that perfectly suited the berserker I was, yes, but it certainly wasn't without justification. The notion that human beings have created a noisy, non-stop avalanche of sensory experience for themselves is tough to dispute, and it is just as hard to dispute its alienating, destructive downside.

There have always been attempts to contain the floodwaters of stimulation, the best known remnant of those attempts being the idea of the Sabbath, the day of rest. The idea that there could be a temporary refuge from the aggressive world of human sound and fury. But even at its best, the Sabbath has become an increasingly flimsy, formalized, self-conscious partition that offers little resistance to the headlong momentum of the human hamster wheel. For the most part it has been swept away in the tide, just another day, another chance to get a great deal on a car or a mattress.

My fasting was a response to that sound and fury, in some ways an unconscious attempt to create a portable Sabbath, a quiet emptiness, a space of pure potential, a Holy of Holies in the temple, a place where mystery could live. But when I began limiting what I ate, things didn't get quieter and emptier. At least initially, they got louder. I wasn't just coping with normal confusion and resistance to such deprivation, but with dark, powerful Catholic notions, too; ideas present in some shadowy form since childhood, when all those tales of ascetic anchorites and saints had been held up as examples of perfection. Did this toxic psychological residue include a desire to hurt myself, to punish myself for being so imperfect? Very likely. Guilt and shame looking for redemption in all the wrong places. But at the same time it's impossible to dismiss the presence of a longing for something truer, more fulfilling and beautiful, like a parched throat craving water.

The clearest expression of both the danger and promise of fasting was an anecdote from the purple book, in which a teacher sits opposite a devotee and places a cup of tea between them. He asks the devotee, "Would you like to have the tea?" The devotee responds that he would, yes. The teacher says, "Don't take it."

To my mind at least, this story revealed another angle: fasting as a means to freedom. Before this, all I could see was the connection between society's obsession with eating (fast food on every corner!) and the survival fears that create unbreakable chains of "necessities"—keeping a job, earning money, paying for food and shelter—which, as I looked at the world around me, appeared to be nothing more than a form of slavery. To get beyond this was the key to being free. If I could manage not to react to the network of fears that easily took my thoughts from loss of job to starving in the streets, then freedom was possible. In my mind, at that moment, it meant getting out from under the tyranny of food.

I also reasoned that eating less was a way to get the attention of my whole being. Hunger as one-pointedness. There is certainly a moment when food stops being nourishment and instead becomes a sedative. I needed to be awake.

With all the various meanings I found in fasting, here's what I did not see: that it could become its own obsession, its own drug.

In the month after Jess moved out, we saw each other a few times and talked on the phone twice a week. She was chirpy and nervous on those calls, explaining how busy she was. I said little, readily accepting her slow disappearance into student life as I settled deeper into the intensity of solitude.

It was in mid-September that I got an odd call from her. It was late enough that she woke me from a sound sleep. I thought something terrible had happened. She told me that she and her roommate Emily were going to a talk by a Sufi master the following Sunday, there at the campus. Was I interested? I had never heard of the Sufis. She described them as the mystic wing of Islam, saying that the speaker was the head of the Sufi Order in America. Whatever that was.

My interest was about as casual as it could be, but I agreed to go, if just to see her. My skepticism about gurus and masters was as strong as ever, fed by observing the odd collection of them that flooded America in those years, offering to take away both your pain and your money. Anyway, the purple book and Mr. K seemed like a full plate to me, and I wasn't looking for a spot in the spiritual buffet line.

On Sunday morning I drove up to the college and met the two of them in front of the administration building. Jess had brought a cushion for me, saying that everyone sat on the floor for these gigs. With about a hundred and fifty others, we were herded into a lecture hall empty of chairs. So many beards and beads among the men, so many shawls and India Imports fabric dresses among the women. A robust cloud of patchouli hovered over us.

We sat down in the very back of the room, feeling a little intimidated by these people, nearly all of them young and infinitely more Sufi than we were. Jess and Emily sat in front of me; I had the wall at my back. A flier identified the speaker as Pir Vilayat Inayat Khan, who had apparently inherited the mission of his father, which was to bring the Sufi message to Europe and the United States. There was a lot more biography to read, but it looked like too much work. I just sat and listened.

Pir Vilayat's face was dignified and handsome, with caramel-colored skin and aquiline nose. Dark eyebrows contrasted with salt-and-pepper hair and a short-cropped white beard. His butternut robes looked Indian. With its slight English accent, his gentle voice was perfectly amplified by a good sound system. The most striking thing about him was his eyes. Retinas as dark as the pupils. Even I, who wasn't paying much attention, could sense the enormous energy flashing from them.

The talk lasted nearly two hours. I remember none of it. I was tired out from juggling my work schedule, my sitting meditation and yoga, and gardening. Sometime during the last half hour, I closed my eyes and leaned back against the wall. As I sat, not really caring what was going on, just letting myself float, something odd happened. The man's voice was suddenly coming not from the speakers near the stage, but from, well, *inside my head*. I sat up, startled, but the voice kept on, inside my brain. When I thought, "What the hell?" his voice was again reaching my ears from the speakers.

I was a little frightened. This was outside of my experience, definitely not *under control*. It was "real," sure, but what did that mean? I was not so paranoid as to think it was a CIA plot or anything, but I did wonder if this Pir Vilayat character was practicing some kind of sinister mind control. He did have those *eyes*, after all. I had to drop that line of thinking, finally, if only because the whole environment of the talk felt better than that. The guy did not come off as a hustler.

We barely spoke on the walk back to the girls' dorm. It felt comfortable. I didn't mention the voice inside my head, but when Emily said Pir Vilayat would be speaking again, in late October, this time at Lone Mountain College in the City, I knew there was no chance I would skip it.

Quitting my job a week later was an abrupt move, but not a drastic one—to me, anyway. I had been steadily moving away from what was considered "normal," and wasn't afraid. It was true it would have been much easier at that point had I decided to become a priest or a monk, someone with an identity sanctioned by society, a title reassuring to observers. But I wasn't interested in reassuring anyone. And I wasn't about to sign on to any organized belief system when my passion rested completely in whatever I could discover for myself. Accepting rote, regurgitated, second-hand "faith" seemed much less sane than anything I was doing.

I couldn't miss the thick ironies of my history, including a father who joined the junior seminary at age sixteen, but had the good sense to bolt when his spiritual advisor suggested that they take a shower together. A decision with serious implications for my existence.

Abandoning the priesthood did not stop my father from being a brooding, conflicted, dedicated Catholic, many of whose lifelong friends were Jesuit priests. I always assumed he gravitated toward Jesuits because they represented the kind of urbane, intellectual spirituality that appealed to him. That, and because, like him, many of them were serious drinkers. As a child, I was accustomed to seeing two or three tables of contract bridge in our living room on weekends, almost all the guests being Jesuits in black slacks and Hawaiian shirts, drinking serious volumes of scotch. It was hard not to be mildly scandalized when I witnessed my parents and several priests acting out some of the big production numbers from *Hello Dolly* or *Mame*. The music was loud, the choreography flamboyant.

Only a few years later, some of these same priests sat at our dinner table insisting to my parents that I would make an excellent Jesuit. I noticed that no one asked for my opinion.

As soon as I left my job, I sold all my wine. It was not like I had truckloads of the stuff; there were maybe a hundred and fifty bottles that would really matter to a wine geek. Yet the rationale was clear enough: Now that I wasn't working, there were plenty of uses for the money, and, more to the point, I had stopped caring. I looked at the various beautiful labels and marveled at the fact that I had so relished ownership of them. I shocked myself into laughter as I realized these bottles were full of grape juice on the way to being vinegar. As the purple book said about powerful desires for things that come and go—"What a strange place to get stuck!" It wasn't that I was disdainful toward wine, but more disconnected from it. My last, most exquisite connection to the world of sensory experience had become irrelevant.

My plan was to offer it to a couple of wine shops—including Brannigan's—but I realized I couldn't do that until George and Miles had a crack at it. It would be a major moment, I knew. Telling them I was selling my most highly-prized possessions communicated a lot about how radically I was changing. They had been completely accepting of what they called my "interest in eastern religions," but would they be able to stand by as I jettisoned my best wines and not declare me criminally insane? Even if the wines ended up in their custody?

They were predictably incredulous. What aliens had snatched the real Paul and left this look-alike zombie behind? But in the end, they bought everything I had.

With his wry wit, George dubbed the transaction "The Renunciation Sale."

A week later, they brought cash to the house and we loaded the wines into their truck. As they pulled away, they were saying "We'll call you," and I chimed in "Yeah, great, of course," but there was sadness in the air. I never felt I was rejecting my friends, and I don't believe they considered for a moment cutting off contact with me, yet we could all feel the tremors, and we knew the earth had moved. Did they think I was crazy? Maybe. Did they think I felt superior to them, so "spiritual'? Possibly. I let all of it go by.

In the two days before the Sufi master's talk at Lone Mountain, I decided I would eat and drink nothing, telling myself it was just another demonstration of one-pointedness. That first night the weather had turned cooler, and when I got up to sit in the dark I felt the cold especially keenly. Still, when I walked into the living room I didn't shrink from it or throw my blanket around me right away; I stood still for a few minutes, letting myself absorb the sensation of cold, completely. It was a new experience. I sensed I was knowing "cold" for the first time—not as a word or an idea, but a mysterious and immediate force. I merged with it in a way that made it impossible to distinguish where "I" left off and "cold" began.

As I sat, it became another of those then almost routine moments when some combination of desire, desperation, and stubbornness kicked in and anchored me in my awkward cross-legged position. It wasn't just that I refused to allow the pain to dictate to me, but also the feeling—one I had had before—of being tired of running away from the present moment, from whatever it was I was avoiding. I might as well give up and take a stand somewhere. Say, maybe *here*, right on this spot on the carpet in the living room of the little house. It made me think of Jonah's attempts to escape the whale, fleeing his encounter with God. I thought: Let's get it over with, then. Let's get swallowed.

Doing my yoga postures in the morning I felt a little dizzy. My mind was quiet and I went through them as I normally did—and as the purple book advised—holding each posture as long as was comfortable. When I got to the third one, called The Triangle, which involves holding legs and torso straight and raising them off the ground with the tailbone as fulcrum—never an easy one—I realized with a shock that I had been holding it for what must have been a full minute. It was even more shocking to realize I could have held it indefinitely. At that moment came a thought, in a voice I knew was not mine: *"Did you think it would not work?"* I acknowledged this startling moment as something expected, as if it were a matter of course.

During that day my stomach often knotted up, but I did deep breathing each time until the feeling passed. I took a shorter walk than usual and went to bed just as the sun was going down. When I woke up as I normally did, around 2 a.m., my breathing was more like wheezing, and my mouth was very dry. Fatigue and weakness made it hard to maintain the cross-legged meditation posture. Before going back to bed, I went into the bathroom and turned on the light. In the mirror I saw an unshaven, gaunt, startled young man whose features seemed immovable, chiseled in stone. As if to negate that impression, I opened my mouth and stuck out my tongue. It was then I realized it had become swollen from dehydration. There was no shock or horror in that perception, but only a wordless, objective notation. In retrospect, if I am theorizing about my mental condition, I might say I was poised to enter the state of No One There. I might say I was someone faintly pleased to have outrun his nature and found himself in a place few people ever go. I might say my compulsion to punish myself was kicking into high gear. Or I might say something else, equally incomplete or misleading. The facts say only that I took a few sips of water.

14.

The notion of anyone, Sufi master or not, "passing into the consciousness" of another person is heavily freighted. First, what did it actually mean? And why would he do it? On that fall afternoon at Lone Mountain College, none of it mattered to me. Though I heard Pir Vilayat's pronouncement that he was going to do this for each of us there in that hall, my world had been reduced, as was so often the case in those days, to little but the blinding physical strain of my poorly-executed meditation position, cross-legged on the floor. That day, I justified myself by thinking that, out of respect, I wouldn't relax my position until he had finished, but in truth it was just more of the fiery endurance test I knew so well. Another round of the wild cocktail that regularly surged into my bloodstream, faithful to my father's genetic recipe.

The silence in the hall was complete. No sporadic coughs or rustling noises from the assembled group. Even the ticking of the radiators had stopped. A few minutes went by, and my attention sank back into the fire of my howling muscles.

A bright light sprang up somewhere behind my eyes. Or under my eyelids. I had no real idea of the source, but I was bathed in light brilliant and effulgent and unexpected enough to distract me from my physical strain. A few moments later I heard Pir Vilayat's voice coming through the sound system. "Don't hunch your shoulders," he said gently.

There was a loud crack—at least it was plenty loud to me—and something between my shoulder blades let go. I lost track of everything, spinning off into a confusing kind of radiance, my senses unmoored, my perceptions a breathtaking jumble coming to me through new and indefinable channels. I felt emptied and filled at the same time. It was as if the membrane that held my self, that had given it shape, had burst and allowed my essence to drift free in the cosmos, without boundaries. I'm sure I would have been afraid, but fear had nowhere to lodge.

Trying to describe this incident later, I came up against the problem I had with other such extraordinary moments: they were so unknown, so removed from my previous understanding, that in each case the language I used to describe them said more about me as a package of past experiences than about the incident itself. My description was bound to be just a Rorschach test for myself—and ultimately for a reader as well.

Then Pir Vilayat did what I later discovered he so often did at the end of a meditation: he leaned into the microphone, exhaled slowly with a tremor in his breath which only hinted at the hard work he had been doing, and in a majestically calm, quiet voice said, "All right." Everyone shifted in their places, took their own deep breaths, and in another few minutes the seminar was over. People stood, gathered their belongings, whispered a few words to their companions as they made for the exits.

I opened my eyes and realized I must have had tears running down my cheeks for some time. I rubbed my face, embarrassed. Though I was free to release myself from my cross-legged position, I noticed I wasn't in a hurry. Odd that when I finally did move, it wasn't just relief that I felt, but regret too, as if I were leaving a wonderful place I would miss terribly.

Just outside the entrance, I stood dazed in the cool sunshine. Jess and Emily looked at me tentatively. Jess asked, "Are you okay?"

My answer was: "I can't believe this man has so much love in him."

My astonishment lay not so much in awareness of my undeniable connection to this person whom a couple of weeks before I would have seen as some bearded weirdo with a delusional religious fixation, but in feeling the reality and power of this thing I immediately knew to be Love. It was something I had never felt before. I couldn't categorize it.

I began an even more intense period of fasting and sitting. Having established a fated connection between ferocious ascetic practices and the state I had experienced at Pir Vilayat's talk, how could I not push harder? Why just dip my little toe in the ocean of new life I had experienced, when I could go headfirst off the diving tower? I saw whatever I did now as preparation for the next meeting with Pir Vilayat, in two weeks' time, a meeting I knew about only because Jess had heard the announcement at the end of the Lone Mountain talk, when I had been in no condition to hear anything. It would be a six-day retreat, daytime only, held at the Sufi House in San Anselmo. It was billed as an in-depth look at the teachings of Pir Vilayat's father. I would have gone if he were teaching us how to make Jello salad molds.

I mailed a check for fifty-five dollars. It was a lot of money, but not going did not enter my mind. *Six days* with Pir Vilayat? I could hardly believe my good luck.

Immediately after Lone Mountain, in my stunned and blissful state, I'm not sure I should have driven home by myself. When I arrived, I took off my clothes and lay down on the floor, meaning to do some yoga postures. For no good reason, I silently began repeating the mantra I remembered from the purple book: *Aum Mane Padme Hum*. I fell asleep quickly and awakened a little after 2 a.m., spooked by the idea that the mantra had taken on a life of its own, still repeating in my head, with a chorus of guttural voices seeming to have joined in. I would have been more frightened had I not believed that anything was possible now that the connection with Pir Vilayat had been made. Whatever it might mean.

I sat down on my cushion and wrapped myself in my mother's crocheted throw. The mantra continued for what must have been an hour, until my legs and back began complaining in earnest.

A passionate, pleading voice finally interrupted the mantra. "Why? Why are you doing these painful things to yourself?"

Another voice, equally passionate, answered: "I am truly sorry. I know it is difficult."

"But *why*? What is the *reason*?"

After all the dead-earnest urgency, there was a moment of silence. And then: "Because the harmony of the universe requires it."

That sweeping and grandiose notion, had it appeared in my mind a few years before, would have made me laugh. At that moment, it was truth.

In the morning I was aware I had lost the standard Voice-Over Narrator that normally held together the "History of Me" story line in my head. Its disappearance wasn't absolute. A commentary or judgment would sometimes materialize and drift through my mind, then silence again, the pool of still water. My internal gaze continually returned to its new focus: the sweeping, endless horizon of Light, a breathtaking dimension most often obscured for us—and by us— through the narrator's crucial placement of people and objects, imaginings and memories, in the mind's line of sight. I sensed that these large and small obstacles we choose for ourselves are there to help us learn. In that sense they're vital. Yet whatever they are, in each of our individual cases, they all have one thing in common: they tend to block the Light. What makes it a real bitch to write down any of this becomes pretty clear. In the land of the written word, without the narrator there is nothing. No one to block the Light and cast a shadow, no one to describe to us the things we need and want to see.

What could be more annoying than being surrounded by nothing but Light if you're trying to maintain a narrative?

During those days, swept along as I was by surges of awe and gratitude—a kind of reverence, really—I mostly experienced hunger as an automatic response at what would have been mealtimes. My diet included a mug of tea in the morning, a slice of toast with cottage cheese and chives in the afternoon, and tea again in the evening.

One morning I was feeling my hunger keenly—a sick, sinking feeling that seemed to collapse my entire body around my stomach. It was time for my mug of tea. As I walked into the kitchen, the Narrator was validating my plan, telling me I was entitled to the mug of tea because its sheer modesty made it acceptable. But then I also heard: Do you want the tea? Don't take it.

Opening the cupboard and being greeted with the smoky, spicy perfume of the Keemun tea I kept there, saliva flooded my mouth. Something inside me was pleading, but I couldn't let myself listen. Was I going to be a slave to this tea? My hands shook as I took the pink ceramic teapot out of the cupboard. When I saw this—hands trembling enough to rattle the lid of the pot—what I was perceiving was the power of the tea over me. My desire to have it filled the whole world at that moment, and it felt completely wrong. I wanted to be attuned to the Light, to the all-engulfing majestic universe, but instead I was fixated on a sip of tea. I couldn't let it happen.

Hands shaking still, I gripped the teapot tightly as I replaced it in the cupboard and closed the door. The bleakness and desperation of that move were matched only by my steely resolve to be free. I turned and took the four steps to the threshold of the living room. I fell

to my knees. It was then that a powerful explosion deto-
nated in my chest, flaring upward through my brain like
a lit match meeting volatile fumes.

There was no one and nothing for a few moments.
Just the stunned, singed, absolutely silent aftermath of
fire. Then a thought: "I don't know what I'm doing."

Everything was different after that.

From the moment I stood up in the doorway, I felt a
fluidity, a physical harmony, an expansive quality in me
that translated to what I eventually realized was "Joy."
In the bathroom mirror later, I saw that my facial muscles had released so much tension that I actually looked
different. I suddenly knew how to smile. Not the frozen,
awkward imitation I usually delivered for the cameras
of family and friends, but a full, whole-hearted smile. I
could feel warmth and energy pour out of my face. This
Joy was not pleasure or even happiness, because it had
no opposite. Joy could not be touched by "un-Joy." It
just was. It just is.

I felt *relaxed*. Somewhere in my consciousness, I
knew I had never known the meaning of that word before. It was definitely not "Sit back, relax, and enjoy the
show" or "Why not take a relaxing cruise this summer?"
Because I was completely present, in that place at that
moment, there was no tension about what would happen next, nor about anything that had happened in the
past. Because I was right there, right then, everything
was incredibly beautiful, too—especially the light. It
was an overcast day, and I watched with amazement as
the diffuse sunlight illuminated *everything in my sight*. I
couldn't get over it.

The narrator still showed up from time to time,

but sporadically and without claws and fangs. Most of the time there was just the flow of events and the time that carried them. There was the curious sound of my breath—which was slow and deep and audible—actually loud in my ears—when I was sitting.

When I went down to the supermarket to get cottage cheese or tea, I had to maintain my role as customer, though I was swept up in a tide of affection for the guy at the register. We had done this routine so many times before, ("Find everything okay?" "I sure did, thanks.") but now I was suddenly aware of his tremendous earnestness, the attempted poker face that revealed his life struggles. The courage and good will in him that sometimes flickered but never disappeared. The whiff of bitterness and self-pity that arose from the times he felt horribly wronged. I had to restrain myself from walking around the counter and giving him a hug. Coming from a family for whom physical expressions of affection were unicorn sightings, this urge was like rivers running backwards. This was how *everyone* looked. I always use the word sparingly, but: Love was what I felt for the people around me. A passionate solidarity with them in the strange and unknowable experience we were sharing, the intimacy of being alive on this planet at the same time. I saw that, in the cosmic scheme, it was like everyone being happy to use the same toothbrush.

Just like the words "joy" and "love," there were others whose meanings shifted seismically. One of these was "peace." As I sat in meditation, I saw that "war" and "violence" were clearly not its opposite. Peace became an ineffable state of being that is part of the Present Moment. It is fulfillment without achievement, grandeur without aggrandizement. Another thing about peace: I saw that I had never really wanted it. I wanted societal order, I wanted undisturbed quiet, I wanted civil obedience—but not peace. And I saw that that was okay, as long as I wasn't hopelessly hypocritical about it. I saw that most of us don't come to this planet to be peaceful. We come here to rock and roll, to mix it up, to learn lessons, to get into the grit of this life. To understand the physics, the psychology, the chemistry of living. For most of us, this life is a huge laboratory class on Separate Creaturehood, not a seminar on Silence.

15.

This is probably a reasonable moment to mention Kundalini. During my college years, I had heard the word in passing, but until the purple book came along it might just as well have been a pasta dish or a family of circus trapeze performers. Even in the purple book, not much was said about it. The only mention I ever recalled was in a section about the use of psychedelics, and since I had used those just twice, I paid little attention. It couldn't have much to do with me. The ominous bit was asterisked at the bottom of one of the pages: "Kundalini yoga is a powerful method, and should be undertaken only under the guidance of a competent teacher."

For whatever reason, I chose not to hear the clear message: Don't try this at home.

Though my education eventually provided me with haphazard snippets of information about a few yoga disciplines, Kundalini remained essentially a blank. Whatever thin familiarity I had with yoga in general I used only as a kind of social currency, the cultural equivalent of a secret handshake, while deep down feeling mild condescension toward it. There were only two types that I knew anything about, actually: Hatha yoga—which I saw as the equivalent of a physical fitness class—and Tantra yoga, which looked like a great excuse to have lots of sex while on your way to attaining Enlightenment, whatever that was. The former sounded too much like work; the latter, viewed through the funhouse mirror of my Catholic brain, was a hilarious, embarrassing twofer that might as well have been called debauchery yoga. By extension I saw all yogas as anthropological specimens of an ancient, backward culture, and certainly nothing that could have serious, lasting effects on a rational, modern person.

If you're a fan of understatement, let's just say that, when applied to Kundalini yoga, my misapprehension was extremely unfortunate.

So what is Kundalini? The short version is that it's a powerful energy, described by Hindu tradition as a serpent coiled at the base of the spine. By engaging in certain practices, a person can raise that energy through seven centers (or *chakras*) located along the spine, and so reach the extraordinary, transcendent state known as Illumination or Enlightenment, when the energy finds its way to the seventh *chakra*, just above the crown of the head. There are loads of esoteric details involved in this exquisite system, but that is the heart of it. At the end of 1974, I had no notion that much of what I was doing was Kundalini yoga, but in fact it almost certainly was.

These were the atomic weapons I was playing with.

It was not smart. But at age twenty-five, it seemed

clear that "smart" was unimportant. Smart was just "being cagey," "playing your cards right," and "looking after number one." I was sure that passion and dedication would trump "smart" every time. This was not smart. Later, when things unraveled, I would tell myself earnestly and often (and as a kind of defensive recrimination against the universe) that everything I did was done with only the highest and best possible intentions.

But I am not there yet. There is still more to tell before getting into exactly what radiation burns look like.

During that time, I walked around in my strange and joyful condition, overwhelmed by a world of greater dimension and space and subtlety—and even humor—than I ever imagined possible. It was as if my nervous system was constantly flooded with exquisite vibrations of some unearthly music. I couldn't have said whether it moved like lightning or at the pace of a flower blooming, but thought and emotion were too heavy to keep up. Only the lightness of being was agile enough to dance to it. It was hilarious and heart-rending, it was goofy and majestic. And it was everywhere.

In the week prior to the Sufi seminar, George called. He asked me to dinner that Saturday, and to see if Jessie would come, too. I hadn't spoken to George, Miles, or Dinah since the Renunciation Sale, and was concerned that whatever I was doing in meditation might leak out all over them and make them uncomfortable.

"I'm not eating much at all, these days, George." I said.

"Man, we don't care what you're eating! If you're

a fucking breath-tarian or something, that's fine—just come over and *breathe* with us. C'mon!"

I laughed, agreeing to come and to enlist Jess if I could. I felt a surge of affection for my friends, enough that whatever awkwardness might come of a dinner together would be outweighed by the joy of seeing them.

When I called Jess, she was wary. Was my voice different? She knew nothing of my freshly-exploded universe, and I knew explanations were impossible. She told me she was all wrapped up with course work. I suggested that if she couldn't come for dinner, maybe I could come up the next day to see her for a couple of hours. She was fine with that.

Seeing her, I was pierced right through by her sweetness, her earnest and demure side which was matched by the tomboy in her, which came out with a "What the fuck?" when you least expected it. Though my heart swelled, I was aware that my response was no longer even vaguely romantic. It was barely personal. All my inner turmoil about our relationship—her seeming disappointment with me, and my uneasiness about her place in my life—had melted away. My feelings had shifted somehow to a kind of intimate identification, where feather-light love met her inside her own heart. I felt the wonder of it, this impossible fusion that made her infinitely more beautiful than someone I might want something from, a person whose body or personality might have attracted me in my old mindset. I could feel how unusual, how radical my response was, but I was not surprised by it because it was so clearly *right*—like a crucial piece of a jigsaw puzzle you've been looking for, one that fits perfectly.

She approached me with a shade of hesitation, wary of my changed manner, my uncharacteristic whole-hearted smile. I told her there was an ongoing process set in motion by my contact with Pir Vilayat, but that it was beyond me to say much about it. We made an afternoon of it, going to Macy's for a few new towels she needed and eating cheese pizza at the mall's food court. I couldn't help but notice her unease through it all.

Before I left, she unburdened herself about what she saw as her failure to be able to meditate. "Maybe I'm just not cut out for this stuff."

"If it isn't important for you right now, then *don't do it*," I said. "It's way better to do what you've got to do, in your own time. You remember that great line from the purple book: You can't rip the skin off the snake."

"Don't feed me that junk."

"Okay, I won't. Though it turns out to be an excellent diet."

She looked forlorn, and annoyed, too. "How weird is it that I would kind of like to go to Pir Vilayat's seminar? But I know I can't! I don't have the time—even if I did have the money. I'm going to *school*. For some reason." Her eyes filled with tears that spilled down her cheeks. With terrible sorrow in her eyes, she asked, "Why is it so *hard*?"

I felt myself go right out to meet her pain, though I knew there was nothing I could do about it. Nothing, except to be there with her.

I gave her the only answer I had: "I don't know."

I reached over to give her a hug, but she pushed me away.

"No! Don't fucking do that! I don't want you doing

118

that! You don't need me, you don't need anyone. What do you care about my little problems? You're 'spiritual' now!" She positively spat that word, then dissolved in tears.

She finally did let me hold her for a minute, until her sobbing subsided. She looked up at me with red eyes and said, sheepishly, "Sorry."

"Nothing to apologize for. I hate to see you hurting."

"And I hate to vomit all this stuff on you. You didn't do anything to deserve this." She looked around the room. "There's never any damn Kleenex around when you need it."

That night, when I woke at 2 a.m., I had Jessie's question in front of my eyes: 'Why is it so hard?' I had no late revelations, no perfect comeback for it. Yet as I let go of the question, I felt lightness and calm settle on me like a gentle mist. I thought of a particularly wonderful quote of Krishnamurti's: "The Problem, if you love it, is as beautiful as the sunset."

Dinner with George, Miles, and Dinah the following night was no less complicated than my afternoon with Jess had been. On the surface, it was like so many dinners we had shared: lots of exotic recipes more or less well-executed, and of course some very good wines. There was George's booming voice, Miles's cool irony, and Dinah's graceful, impeccable hostessing. They had invited another couple, wine enthusiasts whom I knew from a few previous dinners.

I announced as gently as possible that I would go light on wine consumption. Miles looked mock-disgusted as he poured me a splash of Bollinger champagne. I still recall it was the 1966 vintage—and it was excellent.

The sips of wine I took didn't seem to affect me much, but the meat I ate was a different matter.

Since Jess had gone back to school, I had eaten no meat at all, and had no desire for any. When Miles teased me about what I was missing in skipping the platter of rare beef tenderloin, I felt perfectly free to refuse. It was not a big deal. So why did I put a tiny piece on my plate? Possibly to make everyone else at the table more comfortable. Possibly to make myself more comfortable. Or was it because I was curious what effect the meat might have on me, in my blissful state? Whatever the reason, a single bite got my attention. I didn't react visibly as I chewed and swallowed, but I could feel it burning like a hot coal as it passed down through my esophagus and into my stomach. I would have been worried, but I no longer registered anything as a mistake or an error, but rather saw such events as a means to learning. And what I learned at that moment was that I would not take another bite of meat. My body was no longer the same one that had enjoyed so many meals in France, from *haute cuisine* to the simple dinner that had brought me to tears at Sierck-les-Bains a little more than a year before.

As I picked my way through the endless courses of that meal, what was most remarkable to me was the string of responses that my mind, so quiet for many days, dished out to me while I sat there. Such as: Aren't you just a mole, a spy in this group? After all, none of this talk is interesting to you. It is just gibberish that's keeping you from precious hours of meditation. You're just pretending to care. You think you're too good for these people. After all, you're so "holy," like Jess had said.

More interesting than the thoughts themselves was the fact that none of them mattered to me. In fact, it was hard to keep from bursting into laughter, with this peculiarly negative voice, so serious, trying hard to inflict wounds, all the while being so obviously impotent. There was no target to absorb its barbs. Whatever "I" was at that point was too busy being dumbstruck by the act of a gracious universe that had put all these people in a little house, having dinner together, in the middle of Infinity.

Everything was made easier because of my friends' graciousness toward me that night. As we sat down at the table, George asked me politely about what I had been doing. I noticed that everyone went quiet. I told him I was doing some internal exploring, and that I had gone to hear this guy who was a Sufi master and who was the Real Thing, I just knew. I explained what little I knew about the Sufis. George nodded his head, eyes down as he listened; I could sense him trying to accept whatever his crazy friend was doing. Miles looked at me with encouragement. I *felt* these people and their affection for me, while my mind read the subtext. You know: If our friend likes this Sufi stuff, then we're okay with that. It sounds a little crazy, yes, but if it makes him happy, we're in. Just so long as he doesn't get any on the walls, or whatever.

16.

The three days before the seminar were spent slipping into a more and more altered state. It became a feeling of total immersion in the almost painful delight of each moment. Wherever I went, whatever I did, there seemed to be no separation between me and any other person or thing. It was a profound feeling of belonging, of union. The words that emerged in my mind to express this were: "Resting in the bosom of God."

Even now, I would like nothing more than to see this as a time when the "I" disappeared completely, in a kind of merging with Life. But of course it's not true. There was still a scorekeeper there, a sliver of self-awareness that could note these events and store them as a chronology, someone who could collect them like merit badges. If there is going to be a manuscript, someone has to be there to write it. Maybe I was sitting on the rim of the volcano, dangling my feet above the lava, perfectly willing to be burned to a cinder but curious enough to want to describe what I was seeing. The final merging, the immolation, seemed like the inevitable next step;

but maybe a few words of reflection—just a few—in the moments before the leap? If you insist.

The first thing I noticed when I arrived at the house in San Anselmo where Pir Vilayat's retreat was being held was the incense. It was called "Stairway to Paradise," and I thought it must be the official incense of the Sufi Order of the West, because it had been a constant presence at the two previous talks, and now seemed to fill the interior space of the house like something you could grab a handful of. I had not been a fan of strong incense since the days when, as an altar boy serving high mass, I had held the censer while the stuff was spooned onto a burning coal. I nearly suffocated when the smoke spewed up in my face. I always thought of it with horror as a kind of smoldering, industrial-strength men's cologne. On that morning, though, the sweet and spicy floral air didn't slow me down for a second. If this was the smell that this man, this teacher, wanted in his house, I was happy to be breathing it. I felt so full, so quiet, so delighted to be there that I thought I would go incandescent at any moment.

The large meeting room took up most of the downstairs area. Its walls were pure white, with meticulous redwood wainscoting and trim around the large windows that looked out on the wraparound porch and lush greenery beyond. The expanse of pale green carpeting was interrupted by thick columns, also of redwood. Sixty or seventy young people put their cushions down on the floor that morning; there were no chairs anywhere. I sat down, closed my eyes, and breathed deeply. There were only the most muffled sounds in the room—a few whispered words, the padding of stocking feet on the carpet, the rustle of clothing. I had to rein in emotional surges that would have had me crying like a baby. I felt like I had been on some kind of intense, harrowing journey for years, and I had just now reached home. Like I had been living a long, heartbreakingly sad dream and had just awakened. The whole thing could have easily become a song by the Carpenters, a maudlin love-fest, except that all the emotions I felt just drifted through me without a pause. One moment there was something, the next moment nothing. I clung to none of it.

When I opened my eyes, Pir Vilayat was sitting on his cushion, twenty feet from me, adjusting the microphone in front of him. I was transported. I could *feel* this person in me —or was I inside him?—and the torrent of power and love that cascaded from his being. This was potentially one of the scary moments you hear about in the news: Brainwashed cult member signs away all his assets to infamous Eastern Svengali. Possible, except that (a) I knew with certainty that this particular person would never require such a thing, and (b) I had no assets.

He led us into a long meditation, something he would do each morning of the six days. This first one was about detachment, and the importance of withdrawing attention from the physical world in order to meditate. He said something like, "Physical impressions get a hold of us because of our emotional attachment to physical experience, so we must withdraw ourselves with the thought, 'I don't want to be pulled this way and that by all these impressions. I want to be *free*.' Buddhist monks often talk about enshrouding themselves in a zone of silence, placing a sentinel at the doors of perception."

So I sat, surrounded by a zone of silence, feeling like even time had dropped away. As he talked about letting consciousness lift away from the gravity of the earth, surrendering to the longing of the heart for beauty and perfection, I got a taste of why mystic poets so often used the drunkenness metaphor: because this transport beyond physical limits to a sense of well-being and power is in some ways akin to drunkenness. What is different is that the often fist-clenching, manic urgency or sloppy hilarity of being drunk is replaced by an uncanny calm and fulfillment that Pir Vilayat often referred to as "equipoise."

Years later, I would get caught up in the horrible little comparative game of wondering if the "high" I was experiencing then was "higher" than the one the person next to me was having. Was I at fifty percent of Pir Vilayat's high, or sixty? It was worse than getting out a ruler and measuring the penises of a roomful of guys.

On the third day I awoke at about 5 a.m., as usual. Though I was as anxious to get to the seminar as someone meeting his lover, I sat for a while and drifted off—out of my body, out of time. When I came out of it, I was running behind schedule.

Ridiculous that there should have been a traffic jam on a Saturday morning. I knew I was going to be late. Possibly very late. I felt the unreasoning panic of someone being deprived of time with the person he most wants to be with. It was the first time in a long time that I got critical with myself. It was not "You stupid shit" or anything so angry, but more, "Why would you take any chance of losing out on the thing that means more to you than *anything has ever meant*?."

I was only ten minutes late, but to me I might as well have missed half of my life. Worse, when I took off my shoes and came into the room, I saw that nearly all the space was occupied. The only remaining places to put my cushion were out in the entryway or directly behind one of the wooden columns. I would not be able to see Pir Vilayat either way. This was a sharp rebuke. If you think so little of this priceless time, then this is what you will get. Chastened, I put my cushion down behind a pillar and resigned myself to a day of only hearing Pir Vilayat's voice. As soon I as had gotten comfortable with my punishment, a huge peal of laughter rose in my throat. The thought came: "Can it really *matter* whether you can *see* Pir Vilayat? Just knowing he *exists* is more than you could ever have hoped for. And you are now here, in this room with him, hearing his voice! What possible difference whether you see him or not?" I was shaking with laughter, somewhere out of my body. Moments later I noticed that ten or twelve people to my left had shifted their cushions to open a spot in the line of sight of Pir Vilayat. I felt a wave of gratitude, nodding my thanks, but their attention was fixed on him.

17.

When we weren't meditating or doing other practices, Pir Vilayat spoke of some of the major figures who influenced his particular branch of Sufism. The best known of these was Jelaluddin Rumi, the thirteenth-century poet and mystic. The story of his "awakening" might not have been as dramatic as the strike-me-blind, knock-me-to-the-ground moment of Paul of Tarsus, but I responded to it more.

A religious academic whose writings were much revered, Rumi was at work on his greatest masterpiece, a thick manuscript full of lofty spiritual thoughts. Surrounded by his groupie students, he was making his way through a public square when suddenly an ascetic holy-man rushed up to him, wrenched the sheaf of paper from his arms and, before anyone could stop him, threw it into a nearby well. There was a shocked tableau freeze. The mendicant (whose name was Shems Tabriz) held Rumi's glance, and, as the students were about to pounce on him, said, "You have only to say the word and you will have the whole manuscript back. Every page will be dry." Still looking into Shems's eyes, Rumi paused a moment and then said, "No."

Having read a fair number of "spiritual" books, I had to love this story. It took Rumi one second to realize he could spend his whole life reading and writing about transcendence, when what he really wanted was to *be* it. He just needed this crazy holy man to punch his ticket.

This reminded me of the moment when I was still living in Woodside and had gone into a Palo Alto bookstore that had a "Religion/Metaphysical" section the size of a football stadium. As I stood there wondering which of these zillion titles I should buy, I thought, "I could read every single one of these suckers and never get within moonshot distance of any Wisdom. Just as true to say I could read none of them, ever, and be Enlightened."

I can't remember which two books I bought.

Pir Vilayat also spoke about Bayazid Bastami, a ninth-century ascetic who was truly impossible to get cozy with. No sweet poetry here, no love songs, just a lot of white-hot, paradoxical, brilliant writing. He tested the amount of God-presence a human body could withstand and still stay alive, the amount of amperage he could absorb without burning up.

Both my berserker nature and my buried Catholic memories of ascetics and martyrs resonated with his ideas, ones that marked him as a deadly earnest, over-the-edge searcher for God.

> I reached the threshold of nonbeing and soared within it, passing from denial to denial — then I attained the reaches of

deprivation, the threshold of Union, and soared within it by dint of denial, in utter destitution, until I was bereft of deprivation in my abandonment, and was deprived even of my destitution by the sheer denial of denial, and the deprivation of deprivation. Then I attained Union.

Pir Vilayat cautioned that Bastami was only one expression of Realization; he used escape from creation as his means to liberation, not acceptance of his place in it as many other Sufi mystics did. "God says to Bastami, 'You are not strong enough to withstand the solitude of my Unity. You will be annihilated.' And Bastami answers, 'That is exactly what I want.'"

That I didn't see him as utterly insane speaks pretty clearly about my state of mind. I figured he must have been experiencing a much more powerful dose of what I was feeling, so it was completely understandable that he would want to be the first moth into the flame. I wanted to go with him. I thought: Everyone wants to go where the Love is; even if there is a difficult dross-burning process that goes along with it, well, sign me up.

At the end of the seminar's final day, as people began to stir from their cushions, one of Pir Vilayat's assistants took the microphone. He said, "Thanks to you all for being here. Please remember to take all your personal belongings with you. And would those who are to receive initiation please meet on the landing at the top of the stairs in five minutes."

Understand: I had spoken to no one about initiation

into the Order, and certainly no one had brought it up to me. I didn't even know exactly what it was. Yet I didn't hesitate for a second. Initiation? Of course. That's why I was there. It was just a formality, naturally, because I couldn't possibly have been more initiated than I already was.

Up on the landing, I sat on the carpet with eight or nine others, all within a few years of my age. Monitored by one of Pir Vilayat's assistants, each went through a doorway, emerging five or ten minutes later. When I was the only one left on the landing, the assistant came out of the room and gestured. "Please. Come."

It is a fact that I have always been a shy person. As an eight- or nine-year-old, a couple of my friends had to talk very fast to get me to go with them to the Cracker Barrel Market on Van Nuys Boulevard to see Skipper Frank, a local TV cartoon show host, and stand in line to shake his hand. The thought of approaching the skipper and meeting his eye was enough to leave me beet red and trembling. So the idea of entering a room in which I would meet one-on-one with a very powerful spiritual adept should have sent me straight into a catatonic fit. None of that happened. I felt *eager* as I walked through the doorway, eager to spend five minutes with the man for whom at that moment I would have done literally anything.

The room had a polished dark wood floor, and was sparsely furnished. Pir Vilayat was sitting on a simple wooden chair, with another one placed a foot away from his knees, facing him. He seemed much larger up close. His dark eyes held mine as I crossed the room and sat in the chair. The way I saw it at that moment, deluded or not, I was in the presence of God, in the presence of Humanity, and I felt a little tremor as I realized just how powerful this man was. He took both of my hands between his, which were enormous and hot. Not just warm, but hot enough that I normally would have re-coiled from the sensation.

Unsmiling through the entire interview, still his voice was soft and reassuring. In spite of my barely manageable state of transport, I realized he could see me completely, and I didn't care. It was a relief. I had wanted to be proud of my successes and regretful about my failures, but looking into his eyes it was all irrel-evant. I felt light as air.

Beyond being given a few specific chants to perform, I remembered only hearing that I needed to strengthen myself and sharpen the steel of my discernment to cut through the bonds of ignorance. I said nothing at all to him. When a long silence told me the interview was over, I put my palms together in the gesture of prayer, then stood and floated out of the room.

The next morning, when I woke at about five, I did my yoga as usual and settled into meditation. I felt great power in my long, slow breaths. Exhaling, I seemed to be enveloping everything in an ether of beauty and loving-kindness which erased the distinction between my chest cavity and the universe. A subtle warmth spread through my body, and with it an intensified sense of wellbeing. There was a stillness in it that suggested the Buddha—stillness that occupied every point in space and time, a powerful presence everywhere, from the bottom of the ocean to deep space. I sensed these were not emotions, not just because they had no relation to any emotions I knew, but because there was nothing personal in them.

The intensity grew. I was afraid for a moment, feeling I might lose consciousness; I let that go, too. And then: there was a towering column of brilliant, shimmering light and energy pouring down on my head from directly above. I was rapt, overwhelmed and aching with the beauty of this presence. Every molecule of my body was singing. It was days later that I realized there was an existing word in the English language for this experience, and that word was Ecstasy. I had never known its real meaning. Was it like drugs? Not any that I had encountered. Not remotely. Nothing else held even a shadow of the power of this feeling. Sex and orgasm were pale and insipid by comparison.

This was of course not just the wonder of it, but its eventual horror as well.

I sat for I don't know how long in its presence, finally realizing tears were streaming down my face. My chest was about to burst. It was unbearable. The thought came: "This isn't necessary. You don't need to do this, truly. I wouldn't have any less love."

During that day I ate nothing, and never got out of the house. My legs seemed to have extra joints; walking was very complicated. I sat in meditation three, maybe four more times during the day and into the evening, I can't remember. Each time, I was gripped by the cascade of diamond light and energy, consumed with the devastatingly powerful sense of well-being and harmony. I wasn't sure I could withstand it, but I didn't care.

In writing about these experiences—especially these—I collide head-on with the words of the philosopher Ludwig Wittgenstein: "Whereof one cannot speak, thereof one must be silent." I write the description, knowing it is pretty much a doomed enterprise. I might be driven to make the effort by passionate memories of the events, but I am still talking about things that are not talkable. I plow ahead anyway, inadvertently shaping and domesticating the frightening, ecstatic power of the experiences by giving them a story line, a context, a poorly-conceived form to make them recognizable to myself and to a reader. But I have to be clear that I am settling for feeble descriptions that explain nothing. I work with the tools I have, content, in a way, to have learned that the Ineffable is real, and that it can never be co-opted by even the most cleverly arranged bundles of words. Thin consolation, but it will have to do.

At the time, of course, I couldn't possibly see such events as anything but sacred and even holy. They were too uplifting and dazzling to allow for any other interpretation, especially for someone with my Catholic background. Though it was out of the question for me to associate them with anything dark or harmful, in fact they held plenty of dangerous and damaging elements, the greatest of these being the very questionable causal link they silently forged, in my mind and heart, between extreme asceticism and rapture. It was a trap with terrible implications, but how *not* to make the connection at that moment? Virtually everything I had done over the previous two years, including the harshest self-deprivation, had led me to this extraordinary place: a place I had sought with all my might, without knowing exactly where or even what it was. Then it appeared, a state beyond anything I could have imagined, one that wordlessly convinced me that it must have been what mystics and anchorites had experienced down through history. It was so obvious. Even without a mind full of images of Catholic martyrs, desert hermits, and ascetic monks, the link between asceticism and ecstasy would have been difficult to question. As it was, it was unbreakable. And it would take its toll.

18.

I had no visitors except Jolene, who occasionally brought me Tupperware containers of macaroni and cheese or the remnants of a casserole. The look in her eye said she understood.

It had been eight or nine months since I had heard from my parents. I felt no urge to talk to them or—with the exception of Jessie—anyone else. Still, it was a pleasant surprise when, at the beginning of December, my mother called.

"We haven't heard a word from you for a good long while. How are things going? How is work?"

Right. They didn't know about that. "Actually, I quit my job a few months ago, Mom."

"You quit your—"

"Yes, but please don't worry. I've never been better. I need to ask you to trust me on this."

"Well, what happened? What are you doing for money, for God's sake? This doesn't sound good, Son."

I could feel her anxiety. A child of the Great Depression wondering if her son would end up a street person— lost, alone, half-crazy. And after a damn expensive education, too.

"I have enough to get by. I've sold my wine collection to help out."

I heard her gasp. "Oh lord, now I *am* worried. There is nothing that would separate you from those wines, and I know it. What's going on?"

"The thing is, I can't really explain it over the phone. I've had some time to be alone, and it's been a great opportunity to look inside. I'm learning a lot."

Pause. "I'm going to be worried, you know."

"So how are you and Dad?"

Without hesitating, I agreed to drive down to the house in Malibu for Christmas. Because of a second, even more unexpected phone call, from Alan Hooker in Ojai, I would also have a chance to visit with him, his wife Helen, and my old friend Dan Moynier, who had given him my phone number. Alan suggested that I stay a couple of nights with them, and I happily agreed. His voice sounded as buoyant and energetic as I remembered it, and I felt a burst of delight in talking with him.

He said: "You sound good, lad. Very good. Whatever you're doing agrees with you."

Those days were complete and full, everything upside down. The moments themselves were the important thing, not their contents. When the ignition went out on my car, it wasn't an annoying distraction for me, but more a chance to encounter the tow truck driver and the mechanics down in town. Every meeting was significant, every one special. I looked in the eyes of people and saw the whole funhouse—the fears, the desires, the light, the dark. I didn't keep a running mental commentary, because I felt I *was* every bit of it, right along with them. Sometimes there was a knowing look from someone, a conscious exchange. Those really sent me into the ether.

The next Saturday, I called Jessie and told her my plans. She said she was not going to Sacramento for the holidays, but to San Diego instead, to spend time with her mother's relatives. She offered to drop me off in Malibu and pick me up on the 29th.

The drive was a six-hour meditation. What I recall about it was a lot of silence between us; the grinding of Jessie's four-banger Datsun made conversation difficult, anyway. Instead of defaulting to a tense and fidgety travel mode, I sat bolt upright, quietly and restfully unmoving, as the crease in the horizon blossomed into amazing landscapes in which every rock, every patch of weeds, every telephone pole was perfect and fizzing with life. It was as if I were completely still while everything around moved according to a perfect computer simulation.

Now if you have ever driven down Highway 101, you know it can look a lot like hundreds of miles of center-divider oleanders punctuated by huge signs of oil companies and food temples dedicated to deep fat. That day I was so delighted with everything I saw that I was laughing inside. A thought came up, from the purple book: a great teacher up in the Himalayas looks at his student and says, "Can't you see it's all perfect?" The student responds, "Perfect?! This horrible, corrupt world, with all its suffering and ignorance? Perfect?!"

And the teacher sighs and says again, "Can't you see it's perfect?" On that day in 1974, it *was* perfect.

I am already on the record about my family. We were never big on expressions of affection, physical or verbal. We patted each other gingerly on the shoulder, hugged in ways that avoided actual bodily contact, teased each other lavishly, and very occasionally parceled out a compliment. That was our repertoire. So it was unusual when I came into the house with Jessie, put my bag down, and *hugged* my father. It was not a manly bear hug, but I felt myself *supple* for the first time in hugging him. My chest sought out his, and was at the same time not afraid to have him encounter me in that physical way. I felt a moment of recoil in him, then a tentative willingness to be held.

My mother gave me a big buss on the cheek, then hugged me in her own way, stiff but more frankly than my father ever would have. A die-hard hostess by instinct, in the middle of our hug she was looking over my shoulder saying, "And this must be Jessie. Welcome! I hope you have time for a walk on the beach and some supper?" She hugged Jess in that wonderful spontaneous way women have with each other, that men both envy and mock.

Jess did stay for a picture-perfect late afternoon walk on the beach. She left just as it was getting dark, saying she thought she could make it for a late dinner with her family. I walked her out to her car, neither of us speaking. Before she opened the door, she turned to face me with a smile that contained just a touch of puzzlement. "Thanks. I enjoyed meeting your folks."

I could feel her still trying to come to terms with this

new version of her friend Paul. She looked hard at me, and shook her head. "This is the craziest shit."

"It's the absolute best we've got," I said, and I gave her a kiss on the cheek.

She smiled again and sighed. "Have a great Christmas. See you on the twenty-ninth."

I felt such love for her then, though I was aware it probably wasn't the kind of love she wanted or even recognized. Was I deliberately distancing myself from her? There is no simple answer. In my eyes, I was closer to her than ever.

I waved as she drove away, but did not see her wave in return.

I felt none of the emotional burden of historical familial sludge that so often afflicts adult children when visiting their parents. In fact, I was strangely energized, being in familiar surroundings now transformed into magical, unknown territory. Because my sister was celebrating the holiday with her boyfriend's family, the house seemed a little empty; my other sibling, 15-year-old Patrick, was absent much of the time, occupied with friends, surfing and smoking weed. I knew he had had an extremely difficult time navigating life with a sharp-tongued, authoritarian father only recently free of his alcohol habit. Though there was no disguising the scars of their conflicts, I sensed a truce during this time, as well as feeling my mother's relief at not having to assume her usual role of mediator. I made no attempt to inject myself into the drama, but only sat with them, silent inside.

At dinner on Christmas night, I was feeling empty and peaceful. My parents and brother appeared to accept the uncharacteristic silences that now punctuated our time together. There seemed so little that needed saying. I looked out one of the floor-to-ceiling windows that marked the dining area on two sides, and gazed at the dark sweep of the Pacific and the nearly full moon that paved a narrow strip of water with platinum. My eyes settled on a patch of water—who knows how far away?—maybe a half mile or a mile. There was nothing remarkable about that spot; in fact, it would normally have been hard to hold a steady gaze on it. But I was doing it; and, as I looked, felt myself actually *out there*, occupying that anonymous patch of dark water with the moon playing over it, the silence surrounding it. The precious silence of nowhere.

I don't know how long I sat there in that state, but I noticed eventually that there was silence at the table. I brought my attention back from the ocean, smiling at my parents and feeling a little sheepish. After another moment, my father put down his knife and fork, and, looking at me in amazement, said, "You're...you're getting bigger!"

It was not surprising to me that whatever was present there should be powerful enough to catch the attention of my father, a man whose attention was not easily caught. I felt keenly then the need to see Alan Hooker—the person who I felt sure would recognize this state, who could participate in it.

My father had agreed to let me take his old Mercedes up to Ojai on the 26th. As I drove up Highway 1, through the morning sunlight, past strawberry fields and wide stretches of fallow land, up past Oxnard into Ventura, I felt how little energy it took to drive a car. The gentlest pressure on the accelerator, the lightest grip on the wheel. I could just vaguely remember the way driving used to feel, as if my body were trying to power the car's movement. I would hunch forward, tensing every muscle on lane changes and turns, straining my eyes to somehow anticipate what was coming toward me. This experience, too, was now different.

I had no idea what to expect from Alan and Helen's house. Would it be a kind of *zendo*, with spare appointments and a hushed atmosphere? Or a quaint cottage among the orange groves, which were so typical of the Ojai Valley? It turned out to be a modest tract home with two-car attached garage, off-white stucco with blue trim. What distinguished it from its neighbors was the large planting of carefully-tended rose bushes that had replaced the front lawn.

Alan met me at the door, smiling his big infectious grin. "Come on in, lad. You must remember you needn't knock when you come next time."

I put down the overnight bag my father had lent me, and Alan took both of my hands in his. I felt a jolt of energy that I first assumed was emanating from him, realizing after a moment that it was passing between us like electrical current.

My bag stowed in the guest bedroom, we sat down in the back yard, under a patio trellis covered by the gnarled, dormant branches of a venerable wisteria. Next to us was a little pond with a bronze turtle perched on one edge, spouting a thin stream of water, making the simple musical sound that I would always associate with Alan and Helen's home.

"Do you have a sense that this is a very important time for you?" He was suddenly all business.

"I can't say, Alan. I'm not doing much reflecting, really."

"It is tremendous that you are not getting in the way of this, lad. This feels to me like Raja yoga. Are you familiar with it?"

"No, I can't say I am."

"Well, let me just say: yes you are."

As we looked at each other, I felt drunk with the beauty of the moment. There was no need to say anything, but I spoke anyway. "One thing that is both tragic and funny, Alan, is that what is possible is actually much more spectacularly beautiful than most of us will allow ourselves to believe. It appears we are born to experience joy, but are taught to believe that it's just wishful imagining, so we reject it. We end up with the pain and confusion that are so familiar, and even weirdly comfortable." I shook my head slowly, smiling. "And that? Just a bit of thought construction. Words. Whenever I speak, I'm so aware that the description is not the thing described."

Alan nodded and said, "I can't remember the artist's name, but he said, 'It is disastrous to name ourselves.' That's a decent summary of the problem. Names give us familiarity and the power that comes with knowledge, but limit us, in the end, to the known. Krishnamurti often talks about 'freedom from the known.' I recall once when he and I were talking about the prison of thought, mental constructs and so forth, and in the middle of it he stopped, looked hard at me, and very passionately said, 'Break out! Break out, or you'll die in there!'"

I had dinner that night for the first time at his and Helen's restaurant, The Ranch House. It was a singular, astonishing place, with its spare little dining room surrounded by dining terraces that were themselves surrounded by lush gardens, flowing water, and a picture-perfect koi pond. Even on its busiest summer evenings, it was permeated with an atmosphere that could justly be described as peaceful. I marveled at the unique beauty of it, unaware that I would eventually become one of its employees. That the guest room of Alan and Helen's house would be my home for more than two years.

We did not talk one-on-one again until the following morning. When I came out to the dining room at about 6:30, Alan and Helen were at the table already, looking at the LA Times. Helen, whom I had met the night before, was a down-to-earth, practical presence who asked if a half grapefruit was alright with me, since the papayas they had been seeing recently weren't so good. Nothing like the Type-A talker that Alan was, she cleared her place long before Alan and I had finished our tea—not to mention our discussion—and was on to filling the hummingbird feeder and watering houseplants. That morning I learned that breakfast with Alan was not actually about the fresh breads from the restaurant, or the homemade jams, or the interesting blends of tea. It was about hours of discussion with an extraordinary man, and the silences that punctuated those hours.

After hearing him refer so often to Krishnamurti, I asked how and when he came to an understanding of his work.

He chuckled. "I can't say it's a question of understanding it. The process of watching is the beginning and the end of the work. But listen, lad: I should tell you that early on, in the late thirties and forties, I spent years in the organization that Mr. K originally led and ultimately rejected. That was the Theosophical Society, an esoteric group with an elaborate, rigid belief system. I lived in a Theosophical lodge and eventually became president of a three-state federation in the Midwest, headquartered in Ohio. I went around giving talks about the virtues of dogma." He laughed. "You knew, did you, that many years ago—long before I joined up—Mr. K had been the Chosen One of the Theosophists, a sort of messiah figure, until the extraordinary moment in 1929 when he disavowed the whole organization?"

"I did know that, yes. Such a brilliant, radical thing, walking away from adoring followers—from his whole support structure. And to leave them with the extraordinary statement, 'Truth is a pathless land,' one that can't be reached through any set of beliefs or any religion. It must have been like a bolt of lightning."

"Truly so. Knowing nothing of Krishnamurti, I had become a Theosophist in 1937. I eventually learned of Mr. K's existence, of course, but like most loyal Theosophists I tended to treat him as a major phenomenon who was somewhat…wayward. And then it all changed." He shook his head, looking sidelong with the hooded glance I would come to know well. "One night in the spring of 1949, I sat in my usual chair in the commons room of the lodge in Columbus. I decided to read some Krishnamurti. I had done it before, it was interesting, and I thought, 'Why not?' There on the page in front of me was this statement: 'Action from a thought is always false.' I sat there, stunned for a moment, then

closed the book, walked upstairs, and wrote out my res-
ignation from the Society. I left Columbus that night and
went to a remote cabin in the woods, owned by some
friends. I ended up just lying on the floor for days." Alan
sat back in his chair and smiled. "Sorry to bore you with
all this drama, but that was, I believe, the first time I
heard something of the message of Mr. K."

We were silent for a few moments, looking out at
the perfect morning.

"What did you do then?" I asked.

"Honestly, I can't say much about that time. I recall lying on the floor, just letting my life wash over
me until I was essentially emptied out. There was nothing left. It was very cold, and I don't know what would
have happened to me if Helen, who was a member of
the lodge, and our friends Frank and Bennie Noyes had
not brought me food every couple of days. Rumors were
thick back at the lodge, of course. Was it madness? A
nervous breakdown? Would I die? Helen told me about
some of this, but in the unusual state I was in, none of it
could possibly have mattered.

"Frank came to see me then, and asked, 'What do
you want to do?' I told him I wanted to go to California,
to Ojai, where Krishnamurti often wintered. He said he
would go too, and asked when I wanted to leave. I said,
'Right now.' I'll never forget him pausing for a moment
and then saying, 'Would Thursday be all right?'" He
smiled. "And that is how we ended up here, chasing the
paradox of a teacher who refuses to be a teacher."

There were more and more frequent silences. After
one of these, Alan sat back in his chair, smiled gently
and said, "I feel nothing but exaltation."

19.

Back at home, I began driving up to San Francisco twice a week to attend Sufi meetings that had been announced in a mailer. They were held in the garage of a house off Army Street, its floor covered in various rugs and carpet remnants. It was always the same incense, the same prayers, the same twenty or thirty people, many familiar faces from Pir Vilayat's talks. There was a lot of hugging, but I was not part of it. I was nearly invisible, still very much the outsider, without a beard, without beads or a loose-fitting white linen shirt; yet I felt at home. After all, I had sat with some of these people on the landing of the staircase in San Anselmo, waiting for initiation by Pir Vilayat.

Jess's roommate, Emily, had given me a copy of Paramahansa Yogananda's *Autobiography of a Yogi*, a work that was popular at that time. I was impressed by it not for the reasons that the purple book had touched me—lightning bolts of passionate recognition that lifted off the page—but because of the discussion of his "karma," the benefits that flowed to him as a result of what he had supposedly done in past lives.

146

I was impressed enough that when I read about some whimsical, psycho-kinetic tricks that Yogananda had performed as a child, such as directing the flight of a kite to allow him to win a competition, the question appeared in my mind: Why couldn't I do something like that? It was superficial stuff, true, but it wouldn't do any harm to try, right? Completely blind to my weird, meaningless "spiritual" ambition, I left off reading and looked around the room. My eyes went to my little dining table and the votive candle in a clear glass cup that rested on it. Perfect. I would try to levitate it.

But how, exactly? Squint at it like Superman using x-ray vision? Eyes closed and concentrating? This stuff actually went through my head. There were no alarms, no sirens going off, nothing to unmask the stunning pettiness, the cheap self-aggrandizement of it. It seemed like a harmless momentary diversion.

At least I didn't reduce myself to magic-show gestures and incantations.

That night, as I was sitting in meditation, a thought came: I wonder what I'll be in my next life?

The answer was not long in coming. I would often wish with all my might that it had been a different one.

20.

"*It is not for man to be either an angel or a devil, and the would-be angels should realize that, as their ambition succeeds, they evoke hordes of devils to keep the balance.*"

–Alan Watts

I don't remember much about the world as it was in 1975 and '76. I don't know anything about the music that was popular, about movies or television shows or politics. I don't even remember much detail about what I did, day after day, filling the time. This is because I was in Hell. And Hell tends to hold your attention, jealously. Over and over, Hell obliterates sensory data and drags you back to the central and overwhelming loss or failure or pain that burns you, that trumps everything else. It touches that raw, frustrated, bleeding, unbearable place in you where you live with exquisitely designed nightmares that do not permit waking. Hell is surpassingly painful, of course, but strangely boring too, like physical torture would be if you knew it would never actually kill you. Hell teaches the true meaning of despair.

My personal Hell was the inexplicable, lightning-flash loss of Ecstasy. Being robbed of the only thing that had come to matter to me, without being provided the relief of death.

It was an unbearable loss made infinitely worse by the fact that I had gradually come to identify that ecstatic state, something so far beyond my wildest imaginings, as confirmation of —what? Which grandiose description fits best? Salvation? Membership in a sainted elect? Anything along those lines will do. Worst of all, I had come to feel I had earned that state, that it belonged to me.

All of it appears now as an embarrassing and grotesque interpretation of Ecstasy, but one that was in truth fated and inescapable, rooted in my earliest, crudest, Catholic vision of the universe. How could someone like me experience such Ecstasy without marrying it to the notion of Heaven? And how could its loss be anything but Hell? These ideas were as ineradicable as bloodstains on a carpet.

Finding myself in Hell, I was angry—bottomlessly, hysterically angry—but confused as to where to direct the anger. Neither of the two available options looked to provide much possibility of resolution or relief. I could focus on myself as the object of anger; there was a lot of ammunition in that clip. I could rage at myself for failing, for losing the impossibly beautiful peace and fulfillment that had become my reason for taking each breath, that had opened my cautious little heart to the power of Love's passionate infinity; but even more because I had accomplished this without knowing quite how I did it.

My second choice was to rage at God. But the very idea of harboring that kind of anger turned me into an instant hypocrite. After all, Whoever or Whatever it was that had provided me with unimaginable Ecstasy was clearly my ticket back to that state. It wouldn't do to let anything blasphemous creep out from under my mental floorboards. It seemed much wiser and safer (though there is no wisdom, and certainly no safety, in Hell) to adopt a long-suffering, persevering attitude, one that made me appear an unshakeable ally of the Good and the Beautiful, though it looked like I had been thrown to the wolves...by God. So, in my Catholic-haunted mind, I became the Martyr at last.

But I'm way ahead of myself.

It was an early morning in February of 1975. Or maybe it was March. It's strange how panic and shock obliterate chronological details but leave a few precise sensory impressions intact: I remember sitting bolt upright in bed, feeling alarmed, knowing something was very wrong. I was denying and bargaining even before I felt the full tsunami force of the horror, before I acknowledged what was happening. There was no physical pain initially, but the realization that the powerful Ecstasy, with me constantly for months, was now totally gone brought on panic that made breathing difficult. I sat on the edge of the bed, eyes closed, teeth clenched, in some bizarre effort to *will* myself back to my previous state. Behind my eyes, I saw some sort of supernova spewing fiery matter into space, reaching for something, escaping, creating, destroying. I was in a cold sweat as I stood up, shaking uncontrollably, trying to take the ten steps into the living room, thinking

Paul Moser

vaguely—crazily—that in another room I might find
Joy again.

My legs gave out and I hit the floor, prostrate, nose
in the thin carpet. In what must have been just a few seconds, my mind blazed through every possible strategy I
might use to regain that state of exaltation, all the while
knowing it was hopeless. Because I had no yardstick
for this kind of fear and sorrow, all those reactions were
doubled. I was being hurled into a pit of desolation that
was, as far as I knew, bottomless. I might just end up
barking mad. Exactly how much despair can humans
withstand before it kills them? This was not a conscious
question, since it would be a day or two before I could
articulate anything at all, but it was one of the unconscious weights I would carry for the next few years.

And I was afraid of suicide. Though talk of it in my
earlier years had never been more than jocular, I suddenly couldn't rule anything out. The world was no longer recognizable to me, and I was not recognizable to
myself. There were no certainties. I would later say I
never seriously considered suicide, but only because my
meditative experiences had made me intensely aware
that it would solve nothing. If I had thought I could
genuinely have escaped from the Universe by killing
myself, I might have given it a shot. But it was obvious
to me, even shell-shocked by horror and grief, that there
was nothing to do but ride it out.

For a few weeks, my mind recoiled in fear of thought
itself. I could not bear the story line that was emerging in whispered language, already horribly accomplished in reality. I must have done some terrible thing
to merit punishment that was as far beyond my ability

to imagine as the Ecstasy now so bitterly mourned. Was I Lucifer? Had I climbed to the threshold of the Throne Room, forgotten to use the secret handshake or to perform some obeisance I should have known about, and so been tossed into Outer Darkness? Or was I Adam, who under the cosmic radar had briefly found his way back into Eden before being detected, thrown out and seared by the flaming sword of that stern angel at the gates? Was I a bad Jesus imitator who had taken things too far, who had created his own private enlightenment in order to be able to dramatize a proper crucifixion scene, in the end asking with feeling: My God, my God, why hast thou forsaken me? Or was all of this just grandiose garbage, and I was actually a low variety of worm who through some freak metaphysical accident had breached the walls of the outer slums of Heaven and was now going to pay for it with an eternity of vicious recrimination in my mind and hot coals in my body?

My desperate efforts to explain what had happened were doomed to lead back, again and again, to these dark templates, dredged up from the murky Catholic substrate of my consciousness, indelible visions of suffering, guilt, and fear that had been implanted in me before I could read or write. All of them led to only one devastating, iron-clad conclusion: this was Damnation. And that very realization redoubled the shock. This was it. This was what every Christian dreads.

I continued living in the Redwood City house, leaving only to drive to the supermarket, where I felt nothing but shame in buying food that everyone in the store knew I was intent on taking home and eating. The act of eating itself became very painful, not just because my system was in one continuous cramp and food seemed to refuse digestion, but also because of my conviction that feeding myself, this cosmically failed being, was the sheerest waste of food. But it was also painful not to eat, of course. The push-pull involved in deciding whether or not to eat was exhausting in itself, so I ate as little as possible, and always with revulsion, my throat trying to heave up every morsel I tried to swallow.

I managed to sleep only fitfully, a few hours at a stretch, waking each time to re-experience that initial shock of loss and damnation—sweating, heart pounding, more exhausted than when I drifted off. And there were the hot coals. I had to sleep lying on my side, since if I happened to roll on my back and touch the base of my spine to the floor, a rocket of pure white-hot pain shot through me, leaving me curled up and moaning. When after a few minutes I realized I was "enjoying" the shreds of oblivion that followed the explosion in my tailbone, I cursed myself as a masochist.

I never questioned the fiery pain; the connection was so obvious. Of course it burned. Hell is all about fire.

I knew instinctively that the pain had nothing to do with actual physical injury and everything to do with my ascetic practices and the energies that had been unleashed by them. What little I remembered about Kundalini came back to me then, frightening me even more profoundly as I considered the ancient forces I had so blithely experimented with in my lone- wolf quest. There was no point in going to a doctor. Even if I'd wanted to, there were many factors that would have stopped me. Money, for one, though that was a lesser concern. More significant, considering my shakiness, my sweats, my inability to think recognizable thoughts, was the fear of being committed to a mental facility. But beyond all else, there was the shame of it. The feeling of unsalvageable worthlessness paralyzed me. It made even the idea of looking into the eyes of another person unbearable. I could never try to explain my condition to anyone, never let them see it, because I felt so strongly that my failure, my plunge into Hell, was not just disgraceful but part of something too sacred to talk about. No one would understand, and I would somehow be desecrating the Ecstasy and the possibility of recovering it. I had to hold it all inside and struggle on, alone.

I dutifully kept up my meditation practice three times a day. It was dry as ashes. I forced myself to do it, often with literally gritted teeth. It seemed more like a mockery of what had gone before than any sort of brave attempt to soldier through the dark night. I read passages from the purple book, from Pir Vilayat Khan's book *Toward the One*, from my old Penguin edition of selections from the Upanishads. All barren and empty. I went for walks, too, at first, but quickly gave them up when it became too horrible to find myself on streets I had walked in Ecstasy. It was extraordinarily bitter to feel totally cut off from everyone and everything, having felt so connected with all of it in so complete a way. It was as if, after living all my life in a dingy, small cell, I was then released into a spectacular sunny countryside for a few months. Then, with no explanation, I was back in the cell.

I recall lying down on my bed, soaked in dread and horror, too frightened to sob, saying over and over to myself, "What kind of terrible pervert am I?"

It was obvious that I had failed to become whatever it was I needed to become, to accomplish whatever I needed to accomplish. I felt I had let down Pir Vilayat, the man with whom I had had exactly one face-to-face exchange, but whom I saw as a flesh-and-blood example of Love, the man who had shared that Love with me in ways utterly real but unknown to my thought process. I couldn't believe that this person might abandon me, like a coyote leaving his charge to die in the middle of the desert; so it was obvious I had done something to bring this about. *I* must have abandoned *him*, and I was constantly tormented by my inability to identify my deceit or stupidity.

I had few visitors. That made sense to me. Oozing poorly-disguised suffering and self- pity, I was a zero, an empty hole, a car chassis that had been stripped and left in a dusty field. Real people went to showrooms where there were interesting and beautiful things to see. In my own eyes, I was of no further interest. Even Jessie sensed this, and came to visit only once, for about an hour. It was awkward for both of us: she, seeing this poor imitation of her friend and lover, one who tended to stare at the wall and failed to respond to her brave efforts at conversation; and I, feeling a brooding, menacing force in the little house, one that might just swallow her too if she didn't get out. She gave me a hug, crying a little as she left. I cried too, then; it gave me a faint breath of relief. It would be more than five years before I would be able to squeeze out another tear, for any reason. Sensing she was never coming back, I stood behind the closed door, listening to her car start up and back out of the driveway, saying out loud, "As long as it isn't personal. It's not personal. It can't be personal."

I played the scene of that morning over and over again, like a stunned, near-amnesiac returning to the scene of his crime. What had happened? I woke up as I had for months, lying on my back, gently, never having stirred during the night.

But my breathing was not the slow, rich, pulmonary-electric event it had been a few hours earlier. There was a tremor in it, a pleading, a desperation, like the flow of words from the victim of an imminent point-blank execution. It wasn't pain I felt at first, on waking. What was it? Puzzlement maybe: a kind of wordless what-is-this? I sat up. The shock came on quickly—the Ecstasy had slipped away by then, but what was there?—right there, in that heartbeat before the flood of horror closed over my head? In the space between the wasp's sting and the perception of pain? What had I possessed that was then possible to lose? This thing that insisted I could not stay with it, nor it with me? This cruel, brutally indifferent force that had saturated me in rapture and joy for months, but had just left the building? I so much needed a name for it now. When it was roaring through every tissue of my body, names were beside the point, a meaningless detail. But with the ground dropping out from under me, I had to have words—words to give it substance, words I could grasp with my mind, words that would let me remember where I had been and allow me even the thinnest hope of being there again.

I wanted to describe it as "Love." But how could I say I stood up and staggered into the living room to retrieve Love? Insane. What was Love, in the world I knew? Crazy little thing called Love. Love is a many-splendored thing. Gonna give you every inch of my Love. Love me tender. What the world needs now is Love sweet Love. That's Amore.

I wanted to call it "God." But this was no better, and maybe worse. God is good. God made all things. God wants you to be happy. There is no God but God. God damn. God bless you and keep you. The God of the Old Testament. The Gods must be crazy. God bless America. God's wounds! With God on our side. And of course there was: God is Love.

Oboy.

Honestly? I would have called it Truth, Unity, Beauty, Power, or Glory. I would have called it the Ground of my existence. Punch-drunk with the papery booze of words, I would have called it a Tour de Force, the Washday Miracle, or the Best Value for Money, if only it would have returned, burrowed into my chest, fired me with its energy, and let me get on with whatever it was I was meant to do. Because if the only thing in my life that had ever felt really true, really valid and beautiful, was to be taken from me, then everything else was going to be wrong. I was a walking profanity.

21.

My isolation might have gone on longer had I not been completely broke. Being in Hell did not allow me to forget that I owed Jolene two months of back rent, though she was too kind to press me for it. I was vaguely aware of threatening letters from the utility company. Then, on a steamy July night, I got a call from an old co-worker at Brannigan's, who was now running a travel agency specializing in wine tours. Was I interested in leading a month-long tour of major French wine regions? About twenty people on a small bus. All expenses plus a thousand dollars. Departure in mid-September.

I felt queasy. Was this a generous offer from the Universe, to bail me out of my financial dead-end? Or was it a sick joke, designed to rub my nose in what I had loved so much in a previous life but from which I could now hardly be more alienated? I was wreckage, after all: the guy who could barely get up off the floor in the morning. A stern voice in my head said, "Do not do this."

I agreed to go.

The tour taught me that, aside from its other characteristics, Hell is extremely portable.

Years later, I tried to see it from the point of view of the clients—the oil executives, the retired army general, the restaurateurs, and of course the half-dozen doctors. When these people met their guide, they saw a pale, rail-thin young man with a rueful smile, haunted eyes, and a distant, apologetic manner. He was not someone they could warm to immediately, if ever. Oh, he managed the details of the tour reasonably well. He knew how to fend off snotty waiters who detested Americans, especially in groups. He dealt with posh hotel managers' complaints about after-hours noise, drunken behavior, too much wet laundry strung around rooms.

He seemed to know the wines well, and did show some spark of enthusiasm when talking about them, but he seemed so much...elsewhere. So preoccupied, so tense, and yet deflated in some way. Some could not but notice his needy, whipped-puppy side, too, and be irritated by it. Wasn't *he* supposed to be taking care of *us*?

Adding to the normal complications of such a tour, the itinerary included merciless luxury that no normal human constitution could withstand. No day went by without meals at Michelin "starred" restaurants, plentiful visits to brandy or wine producers, and lodging in hotels so exclusive that, on seeing us, they made it clear we would never have been admitted if only they had *known*.

Some clients rebelled and began skipping some of the restaurant meals in favor of simple impromptu picnics. Going to Paul Bocuse for lunch (sea bass *en croute* with *beurre blanc mousseline*!) and Lameloise for dinner (game hen stuffed with truffles and foie gras, veal demi-glace!) might be interesting on a dare, but to endure such meals repeatedly, day after day, was courting disaster. By the time we returned to Paris, three quarters of the clients—and myself— were ill with colds, flu, constipation, or Escoffier's Revenge.

Even in my half-alive condition, I could hardly miss the ironies of all this, far richer even than the meals I had eaten. I was unable to enjoy some of the best food and wine in the world— food that in the past I would have killed to sample—yet was equally unable to return to the Ecstasy that had enveloped me so recently. So I was nowhere. It was easy to hate myself, but extremely hard to be jocular with clients while doing it.

When I returned home, I fell back into lethargy. My mother called, and I let it go to the answering machine. Whatever breezy narrative of the trip I might concoct, I knew she would hear the despair in my voice. I would not talk to her until the following spring.

I did talk to my sister Kris, who had quit her teaching job in San Francisco and gone back to school—at Stanford—to get a Master's in Education. She seemed excited, and asked me to come to dinner at her newly-rented house in Palo Alto. I felt my desire to see her collapse under the weight of my shame, which could bear isolation much more easily than sympathy. I told her I didn't feel up to it.

I also got a call from Alan Hooker, who was jovial, chatty, and energetic. I strained to imitate a relaxed and happy person. My teeth were on edge.

He said, "Listen: I called because I was thinking of

you, and of something that Mr. K said many years ago. He said, 'You are all so busy trying to paint a picture of the life you think you want. Why not let life paint its picture on you?'"

Anything I heard now that pointed to wise courses of action made me feel like I was on the dock, waving to the Ship of Realized Beings as it pulled away from me, headed toward Valhalla. I had to keep up a brave, unenvious smile, watching it become a dot on the horizon. I wanted to say something to Alan about my situation, but couldn't bring myself to do it. It wasn't just that I admired him and did not want to expose him to my failure and disgrace for fear he would reject me; it was that he was one of the few people who had recognized the Ecstasy, and the only one who had met me there when, not even a year before, he had sat back in his chair with a serene smile on his face and said, "I feel nothing but... exaltation." I couldn't let him know about Hell.

"We'll talk again," he said, finally. "Visit when you can." Click. Over time, I learned that Alan never said goodbye.

I resumed driving up to the Sufi Center in San Francisco on Tuesday and Thursday nights. I had no good reason to go, having even less connection with these people now. It was exhausting and, given the cost of gas, a waste of the little money I had. It was not remotely comforting to sit alone in the midst of that clubby group, feeling like a dead zone, a perfect pariah. I must have hoped it would be penance for my sin. Or at least a noble show of will-power, sticking with Sufi disciplines and rituals regardless of results. Saying the prayers, listening to readings—all would have been lifeless and wooden except for the horrible, constant sense of falsehood that saturated the air. I thought: I am the only person who could possibly be a bigger hypocrite than these people.

George and Miles called a few times, inviting me to wine tastings or dinner, but I never responded. I couldn't decide whether they were tempting me, trying to distract me from finding a way to regain Ecstasy—or just well-intentioned friends making a last ditch effort to rescue me from a horror they could not possibly understand. Invariably I went with the former view, though never without the chilling realization that I might be dead wrong.

One steel gray afternoon–November? December?–I was lying on the floor of the living room in a near-fetal position, as I did for hours at a time, a corpse with a pulse. In a half-light of consciousness, I could hear the few cars that breezed past the house. I started when I heard my kitchen door open. Propping myself up on one elbow, I saw George and Miles coming into the living room. They were very serious as they greeted me. I gave them a wan smile.

"What are you guys up to?" My voice was hoarse.

George was carrying an attaché case. "Hey," he said. "We just thought we'd come by for a visit." Miles was wound up like a spring; it was hard to watch him feign casual behavior. They sat down, cross-legged on the floor in front of me, and George snapped open the case. Inside was a bottle of wine, some glasses, a couple of pears, an apple, a paring knife, a corkscrew, and a paper plate. Without a word, George began slicing fruit while Miles laid out the glasses and opened the bottle.

When I saw the dark, smoky color of the glass and the bronze-gold label, I realized this was one of two bottles of rare 1945 Vouvray that I had sold to George as part of the "Renunciation Sale."

I said something like, "Wow, this is so nice of you guys...you didn't have to go to all this trouble...." Neither of them looked at me until they had finished their work and the beautiful, brilliant amber wine had been poured. They raised their glasses, looked at me with tight, determined smiles, and waited for me to pick up the remaining glass.

"Here's to you," George said softly. And then, with deliberate emphasis and a meaningful look: "Here's to good friends." We clinked glasses, and they looked at me with sympathy and pity. I looked back at them wearing a similar expression, because I did pity them. These thoughtful, generous people, wasting their time trying to help someone who was not worth the effort. They might think they had an idea of how it was with me, but they could never know. The gap was too great. It was like calling to each other across the English Channel.

I knew in my mind that the wine was extraordinary, but I felt repelled by it as I took a single sip. My nausea and dizziness might have been the result of hunger and exhaustion, or maybe the shock of a surprise visit. Whatever the reason, I just wanted them to leave. The pain of having my misery observed at such close quarters made me desperate to get back to solitary mourning. I put my glass down. "It's great of you guys to do this, but there's no need, really."

"We think there is." George's brown eyes were almost defiant. "We're here to help a friend."

I just nodded, silent, the sad smile frozen on my face. They ate slices of pear and apple, not looking at each other, and only occasionally at me. They seemed almost sullen.

"What have you been doing?" Miles asked me, looking at his glass of wine.

"Not much. Just feeling like I need to spend time by myself."

George jumped in, almost accusingly. "So you don't see anybody? No friends, no nights out? What about Jessie?"

"Jessie and I have been in touch, but I'd rather not go into details. If you don't mind."

George held up his hands, palms up. "Fine. Great. But we didn't come over just to share some great wine with you. We want you to come over next Friday for a tasting. We're doing '72 Cote de Beaune reds. Just your deal."

"I appreciate it, really. But no thanks."

Miles couldn't restrain himself. "Are you kidding me? We've got Tollot-Beaut *and* Prince de Merode *and* Pousse d'Or! You can't pass this up! Shit, man, if you can't go along with your friends on something great like this, what's left?" George looked at him sidelong, annoyed.

"Well, sometimes it's best just to trust that a friend is doing what he needs to do."

Long uncomfortable silence. They looked at each other. George took the full glass from my hand and toss it down in one gulp. He gathered up the glasses while Miles put the cork in the bottle. At the door, George paused and turned toward me. It seemed like he wanted to say something more.

22.

The days, weeks, and months that followed were framed by a paralysis that was now familiar. The unimaginable had already occurred, but my consciousness could not accept the finality of its doom, and continued to speed through scenario after scenario, searching for one that would explain the horror and restore me to my previous state. The process was not verbal—it was far too fast for that—but more a constant panic just below the surface of the scattered thinking I was able to do.

Looking at every single decision, I couldn't help but try to calculate whether *this* one—the piece of bread I would refuse to eat, the unbearably dry meditation I would tough out, the window I would not close in order to allow myself to be uncomfortably cold—would be the one that would give me back my place in the universe. There was an air of superstition about it. Maybe it was a kind of OCD. It created a steady diet of edgy, constant, exhausting dread. Should I get up at 4 am, or stay in bed? Should I answer the phone? Should I buy the large-size cottage cheese or the small? Should I wash my dishes now, or leave them in the sink? And since none of my decisions restored me to Ecstasy, they must all have been wrong. From when to brush my teeth, to my posture when sitting on the toilet, everything was a mistake. I was the wrong person, doing the wrong thing, at the wrong time, for the wrong reason.

In turn, this led to a complete loss of discrimination, the absence of any capacity to judge what was good or bad for me. It wasn't actually a complete loss, since I would never have done anything harmful to others; but I was certainly willing to do things harmful to myself. If some half-way credible teacher/guru-type had asked me to hurt myself in order to retrieve the lost Ecstasy, I would certainly have done it. So I was very vulnerable to circumstances; anything that happened—a call, a glance, a written word, a chance encounter—could, and often did, change my ship's course. I was like a person hypnotized, one to whom suggestions were constantly being made by my surroundings. No one of them received greater weight than any other, since that kind of discrimination was beyond me. I had no will in any of it. I was a piece of cosmic junk, drifting in space. I often wished I could cry, but for whatever reason could not.

It was my great luck that, after a series of phone calls, my sister Kris succeeded in getting me to come to dinner. She was still loving her graduate classes at Stanford's School of Education and wanted to tell me all about them. I was in a cold sweat at the idea of going, but a wave of remembered affection for her won out.

I call this luck, realizing that in my condition I might

well have dedicated myself for the next twenty years to duck hunting if someone had called me and said, "Why don't you come along? It's a great life. All you need is a good rifle, a few boxes of shells, and a warm coat. It is the true meaning of freedom and contemplation." I might have become a roadie for a rock group, a rabid baseball fan, a hot-air balloonist, or a Mormon. Okay, maybe not a Mormon. That would have been a bit much, even for me.

As it was, my dinner with my sister led to my signing up for the program. Because both professors who interviewed me insisted that a few years of teaching was the best course of action in launching this new career, I made the fateful decision to get a teaching credential as well.

After months of staring into nothingness, repeating to myself, among other desperate mantras, "Give Me a Game Worth Playing," I was bound to see my sister as an oracle. I believed she was carrying a "safe" message for me. It came to me that if I were going to be the wreckage of an abortive attempt at Enlightenment, then the least I could do was to work in the grosser spheres of education, with the hope that whatever had been best in me would rub off on young people. You know: failed boxer becomes corner man for bright young stars who might just rise to the top. It would be a vicarious life of hopeless longing, but at least it was something to *do*.

I believed I was throwing myself into a world of dubious rules and even more dubious goals, yes, but at least there *were* rules and goals, and contact with the world, and a group of people who agreed to share those rules and goals. I mean, they seemed to take it all seriously, so I would try to take it seriously, too. It was a relief of sorts. I felt like I had been given a bowl of the thinnest, most tasteless gruel, but it was my duty to spoon it up, to swallow it and be grateful.

When I applied for a student loan, I treated the skeptical loan officer to an impassioned statement of purpose. I told her I was certain I needed to teach. I had ideas about how to reach young people. When she looked doubtful, I told her she couldn't possibly deprive me of this opportunity because I was certain I could succeed. I shocked myself with how easily I conjured up all that conviction; not only was I uncertain about my vocation as a teacher, I was doubtful I could hold down any job at all. Maybe it was her furrowed brow, her mild suspicion that brought out my persuasive energies. Deep down, I really didn't care what I did. The teaching thing was as good as any other bowl of gruel. I remember thinking often of a story I had heard somewhere about the Dark Ages Irish monk who would climb into a tiny boat at the seashore, set the sails and lie down in the bottom of the thing, determined to go where God wanted him to go. I was stirred by that image because it was so trusting, at once so frightening and so serene, so logical and so nutty. It combined passive and active elements in a strange vision of courage. I felt some kinship with that monk as I signed up for classes, bought books, and began going to classes.

23.

I moved to Palo Alto, where I had found a cheap, seedy apartment on Hamilton Street, part of the upper floor of an old house that had been partitioned into four units. It was a studio which had an odd little kitchenette reached by walking up three stairs. Two paces took you to three descending stairs, at the bottom of which you were met by the bathroom door. The bathroom was nearly as large as the living space, and almost completely covered by a ratty mustard-colored carpet remnant. There was a toilet in one corner, looking embarrassed, and an old claw-footed tub fifteen feet away in another. The sink, hanging on the wall and listing to the left, was between them.

It was a "furnished" apartment, too, including a living room sofa upholstered in greasy polyester tweed, whose springs sounded like some kind of demented harmonica performance when you sat down, and four chairs and a round dining table painted with a thick, sticky, dark stain. To keep my clothes from sticking to the chair seat, I draped a towel over one of them. I never got a bed, having decided to continue sleeping on the floor. I slept on a single blanket, using a second one to cover me.

The place felt like the remains of a house just after a fire: eerie, exhausted, desolate.

Hunger was a constant, partly because I had little money for food, but more because I could still hardly bring myself to eat. The push-pull of the inner battle drove me to devise a not-entirely-intentional form of torture for myself. I would take a walk around Palo Alto, always ending up by The Good Earth Restaurant on University Avenue. As winter moved into spring, its door was often open. Each time I approached, a variation of the same dialogue ran through my mind. ("I think I have enough money to go in and have a sandwich. Yeah, a sandwich, that would be nice. Just a turkey sandwich, with some nice cheese on it, and a big mug of tea. I could do that. Come on. This is not a big deal. Human beings go to restaurants, for God's sake.") Then, at the entrance, anxiety would rise into my throat, choking me. Sometimes I would walk right by, with stiff mechanical steps, deliberately not looking inside. ("I'm not going in there. It's a hassle. Getting a table, dealing with the waiter, why spend the money anyway?) Or I would walk into the restaurant, heart pounding and mouth watering as I looked at the display case next to the cash register—big sloppy cherry danishes, chocolate chip cookies, blueberry muffins the size of a fist. I was being tempted to betray a haunted memory that I could talk to no one about, to give in to my animal nature and anaesthetize myself with a full stomach. ("Maybe I'll just buy a few cookies, maybe a nice muffin for breakfast tomorrow. That'll be cheaper than sitting down and eating here, anyway. Yeah, that's perfect.") More than once I had my wallet out before I was overwhelmed by the intoxicating smells of grains and cheese and meats, along with the pungency of the cinnamon spice tea they served. Ravenous and nauseous and enraged at my inability to be like other people in this seemingly simple activity, I walked out, under the puzzled gazes of the people behind the counter.

I did eat a few meals at that restaurant, but only when accompanied by my sister, whose presence and conversation provided distraction and cover for my act of weakness. Even then I was queasy, never able to eat everything I ordered. I took doggy bags home and threw them in the garbage.

In class, I often had an eerie feeling of invisibility, though my tests and papers were returned to me with comments and grades. I couldn't tell whether students and professors were not looking at me because they could see the horror of my life written all over me and were politely ignoring it, or because they were trying to avoid something threatening and pestilential.

Most evenings when I came home, wrought-up yet exhausted, I forced myself to lie down on the floor and try some yoga *asanas*. When I invariably discovered how painful they were, muscles stretched tight as bow strings, I would give up. I often lay there all night, careful to keep my back arched to avoid the molten heat of my tail bone touching the floor. I slept fitfully, in a half-awake state of frustration and the bitterest despair. I pounded my head rhythmically on the floor for long stretches just to get some release.

Over and over, it was my sister who provided a

footing for me on this nightmarish terrain. Still in her house about a mile from my apartment, she exerted just enough gravitational pull to keep me from drifting into outer space. She became the only human contact that was even remotely bearable, and she did it without ever being aware of what had happened to me. That was the odd thing about my relationship with her: we always seemed to understand one another, but it was rare that we would talk seriously about anything very personal. She was unfailingly sweet, but in a casual, accepting way that could hold no threat for even the most distraught person. Even her haunted, half-mad brother.

Her house was a refuge for me during the summer of 1976, a refuge from the withering, damnation commentary that played in my head when I was alone, the dark vision on which my inner eye constantly rested. Yet my sister seemed able to look past it all. She could make beef stew using our mother's old recipe, chat with me about her classes, theorize about the upcoming presidential election, and somehow manage not to see my despondent self, whimpering silently in front of her.

She played music she liked—Keith Jarrett, Janis Ian—and though I could not bear to hear music in my apartment, being at her place was all the permission I needed to listen and feel some of its soothing effects. She didn't even ask questions when, in helping her do the dishes after dinner, I kept moving away from the sink each time I handed her a dish I had washed. I two-stepped around the little kitchen aimlessly, chattering to distract from my jittery, unnatural moves. Even more than a year after the catastrophe, I could not stand still for any length of time. The fire in my tailbone was especially excruciating when I couldn't continually shift my weight from one leg to the other, or, better yet, keep moving around.

At the end of the summer, when I began student teaching at nearby Valle Verde High School, I discovered what most of my professors already knew: Theorizing about teaching is much more fun than actually doing it. I don't know that the students learned very much about the history of 20th Century Europe, but I learned an important lesson, i.e., that I did not enjoy teaching. The catch was, rather than allowing me to quit, my discovery confirmed my choice. In teaching I had found a means to throw myself away. I might just as well be miserable teaching high school students as being miserable doing something else. It was all the same thin gruel, so eat up. The worse my teaching experience got, the more I subconsciously decided it was a good thing to be doing, since every day was such severe penance. Had I been in a job I truly enjoyed, it would have been unbearable. I would have had to quit.

Another lesson I learned was about my expectations for student behavior. I turned out to be a strict disciplinarian, in imitation of my teachers at Loyola High School in Los Angeles, far away in the smog of time. Injected into the finely-honed, go-along-get-along culture that had evolved at Valle Verde, my rigid notion of discipline was a doomed personal ideal; but I was not going down without a fight.

I was tested at every turn: epidemics of throat clearing, scores of notes passed, rashes of restroom requests, every form of cheating imaginable, and many—oh so many—blank, uncomprehending, faux-innocent stares. Within a few weeks, my response was automatic. I was the Nazi teacher who threw them out of the classroom. If they so much as looked sideways too often, if they seemed to drop their pen or their books too frequently, if they did any of the hundreds of possible disruptive behaviors so many students enjoy, I would tell them to get their things together and get out. I couldn't forgive them for being students, playing the eternal game of cat-and-mouse that characterizes much of high school education, while I clung more or less successfully to sanity. It didn't seem fair. They should have understood. I had to acknowledge then the hopeless chasm between me and these young people. Chronologically, it was only about ten years, but it felt like forever.

Just before my graduation, I visited the placement center to look for a full-fledged teaching job and surprised myself by setting my sights on a Catholic high school in the San Diego area. I had less than no use for the Church, of course, but it had the advantage of being the Devil I knew. And I figured discipline there had to be more serious than in public schools, since kids could actually be expelled if they weren't staying in line, as opposed to public schools that were stuck with problem students forever.

As to the larger questions of why I went into the placement center in the first place, why I flew down to San Diego for an interview, and why I was continuing with teaching at all, I was mostly silent. My only thought was that I needed to earn money to repay the student loans I had pursued so earnestly. I was offered the job, and I took it. It felt like walking the plank.

24.

I had had a few phone conversations with Alan Hooker during the year, so he knew I would be teaching near San Diego in the fall. I accepted his invitation to stop for an overnight visit on my way down, torn between a desire to talk with him and the fear that he would see through my painful cheeriness and begin asking difficult questions. Maybe I was hoping he would. Maybe he could explain what had happened to me, and what I might do to regain the Ecstasy.

When I arrived, Alan put his hands on my shoulders and looked at me searchingly. I was struck again by his natural intensity—large facial features dominated by those hooded, penetrating eyes.

"You look tired, lad." He spoke in a matter-of-fact way. I waited for a serious pronouncement, but instead he said, "I thought we'd go down to the restaurant at six. You have just enough time to freshen up and lie down for a bit if you like."

Just as before, Alan and Helen fed me a fine meal, with excellent wine and conversation.

The next morning, around 7 a.m., I woke with more than my normal jolt of panic. I dreaded imposing on Alan and Helen—these mysterious people I regarded as heroes in the world. But then, I dreaded imposing on anyone at all. I pulled my clothes on and, as I came to the table, put on my most pleasant early morning face, which wasn't very. Alan sat in his chair at the head of the table, wrapped in a fine cream-colored wool robe and sipping tea, looking like a pasha. Helen sat opposite him in her periwinkle velour robe, reading the newspaper. After we had had a thick wedge of Crenshaw melon, toast and tea, Helen got up from the table without a word, as she had on my previous visit, and left Alan and me to talk.

The base of my spine was burning so fiercely I could barely sit in the chair. Alan spoke with contained excitement. "My friend, I must tell you: I woke in the night as I so often do, and there, in front of me, was the most interesting question. What is it that everyone wants? And an answer appeared: We just so dearly want someone to tell us what to do." He smiled and shook his head. "It seems true to me. It's what religion is about. All that stuff. Our need for some kind of certainty overwhelms our willingness to see what is true and real. Does this seem possible to you?"

And we were off, on a fantastic conversational voyage, this time about certainty and belief, larded with bits of Alan's past. He was so animated and alert to every word, prodding me to explore the territory while I, in a cold sweat much of the time because of my spine, was fascinated and stimulated in spite of myself.

"Lying there in bed, I was just so full of laugh, I

176

can tell you. Needing to be right, to be certain. Such a burden to carry! I saw that I have been a prime example of this mischief in the past, just as you have. I couldn't think of a single person who *wasn't* up to his neck in it, in some form. It was high-larious!"

"It sounds more sad than funny, Alan."

He looked at me a little quizzically, still smiling. "My dear friend, faced with a spectacle like this, what else to do but laugh?" And he burst into one of his head-back, uninhibited belly laughs. "You knew I had a teacher when I was living at the Theosophical Lodge in Columbus, did you?" he asked, catching his breath.

"I think you mentioned it once. But who was it? And how did you end up there, anyway?"

"Well, that is a story as long as it is boring, but let's just say I was more thoroughly lost and confused than any man in his thirties has a right to be. I went to an astrologer who looked at my natal chart and asked, 'Why haven't you killed yourself?'" He shook his head. "Anyway, Theosophy gave me plenty of answers—some of them to questions that couldn't possibly matter to anyone. But the real answers I wanted came from Jenny Bollenbacher, who was my teacher and mentor at the lodge until she died in 1947. Oh boy," he chuckled, "Jenny was a real tyrant with that gimlet eye of hers! And she cursed like a sailor. Half German, half Cherokee, and all business when it came to discipline at the lodge. We had very clear, very solemn responsibilities to each other. She provided me with absolute guidance and I made my psychic skills available for development in the name of Theosophy, the Brotherhood of Man, and all the rest of it."

177

"Sorry Alan, but I'm too curious not to ask what you actually did to learn about being a psychic. Were there some kind of practices? And what did you do after you became—I don't know—accomplished, or whatever?"

"I can tell you, it wasn't glamorous or fascinating. It was hard work. What Jenny taught me were mostly techniques for getting my personal self out of the way of phenomena that are more subtle than the ones we call 'reality.' Some techniques were meant to neutralize powerful conventions that limit the human capacity to perceive—like time, or space, or language. These opened up various possibilities for action, many of them difficult for people to accept as real and true. For instance, during World War Two we spent time nearly every day sitting quietly and locating the consciousnesses of soldiers who had died suddenly and violently. They were usually very agitated. We would calm them down, explain that they were dead, and give them instructions about what to expect next. It was very intense and draining, but Jenny saw it as our duty.

"It always sounds strange to speak of these planes, but finding the way through them was what Jenny required. And that was that. You have to understand that these were the days of very traditional relationships between teachers—psychic adepts like Jenny—and students like myself. From the moment I staggered into the lodge to begin life as a resident member, I agreed to do whatever she asked of me. Full stop. I did nothing but washing, cleaning and cooking for the first two years or so—because she told me to. My God, I was miserable!"

"But why didn't you just leave?"

"Because I was sure I was in the right place. And Jenny had agreed to help me develop the psychic ability I knew I had. Or," he added, smiling mischievously, "it might have been because I wanted her to tell me what to do. You will find this hard to accept, but she not only told me when to go out and get a job, but even when it was time for me to marry."

"You're joking."

"Not a bit." He regarded me seriously. "Things are different now. At that time the teacher/student relationship was sacred, very much like the guru/chela commitment. These days, young people strike out on their own, to find their own paths. And that of course has its attractions. But it is a fiery crown you wear, that crown of independence, and it can be a powerful burden." He sat back in his chair, hands clasped on his substantial stomach, looking at me intently. "I could tell *you* what you should do, you know. I could indeed. I know what it is. But I won't." He smiled faintly. "Because you wouldn't do it anyway."

I knew he was right. But my God, it was hard to restrain myself from asking.

Suddenly it was late ("Eleven o'clock already!") and we adjourned to shower and dress—in time for lunch. Being at Alan and Helen's was like being in another world—recognizable but somehow different. It was as if some other currency was used here, as if the traffic signs were different shapes and colors. A place where serious conversation was a priority, and admiring an azalea in full bloom could not be left off the agenda. There was nothing precious and cutesy about it. It was the way you would like things to be but didn't dare hope, for fear it would turn out to be Los Angeles all over again. It was, in its quirky way, magical.

The catch was that it made me feel worse than ever. The ecstatic state clearly belonged here—I didn't. I thought it perfectly just that I not be fated to stay in Ojai. I didn't fit in. There was not enough posturing and phony piety and gut-melting anxiety in Alan's house. Not enough damnation. As I drove away that afternoon, I felt relieved that Alan had not brought up my condition. He told me years later that there was not time then to do anything other than open the wound. It needed more time, more quiet, more attention than a day or two might provide.

That time was yet to come.

25.

It was in my first weeks at Marian High School that I began to get a feel for the actual meaning of the word "blasphemy." My good Catholic education referred to blasphemy as speaking irreverently or profanely about God or things sacred, which was fine as far as it went. You know: high school boy tries to shock and entertain his friends by saying, "Jesus was a gay motherfucker, for sure!" Or whatever. But my view was broadening, now that I could look at the world around me and see nothing but a vast torture chamber, a cesspool of physical, emotional, and psychological suffering or the desperate attempt to escape those things. Seeing everything and everyone as unspeakable manifestations of sadism, I felt the meaning of blasphemy was beginning to emerge. Still, I would never curse the whole thing because that would have meant descending to its level, and I would never stoop to that. Never.

I couldn't accept what I saw around me, couldn't join it, since it frightened and repelled me so completely. I was wildly envious of my fellow teachers, who could be genuinely engaged in conversation in the lounge while they helped themselves to a mug of bad coffee from a cart coated with a dusting of non-dairy creamer, like cocaine at a wild party. There was no place for me in any of it, I knew. So I did my best to pretend, and everyone was very polite about my poorly-disguised pretense. What did they think? Did it matter?

My inner voice had taken up a new, withering criticism: I had been doing this solitaire *Gotterdammerung* for better than two years now, and what was the point? Nobody knew, nobody cared. If only the Ecstasy hadn't been so real. The memory of it stopped me in my tracks, forcing devastating comparisons with whatever was going on at the moment.

I don't like to think what would have happened if Sister Ellen had not appeared.

I was leaving my classroom at the end of the day, no more than a few weeks into the semester. I remember the onshore wind had kicked up; it was unusually cool. I locked the door and began walking down the arcade that ran the length of the building. I'd taken just a few steps when I looked to my left—maybe I'd heard something—where the administrative offices were, along with the teachers' lounge. Fumbling with her keys in front of the lounge door stood a nun. I recognized her as one of the young ones, knee length habit, sensible black shoes, the half-veil set back on her head revealing straight brown hair parted in the middle. She stopped fighting with her keys and raised her right hand in greeting. I looked behind me to see whomever it was she was waving at. No one there. I flushed, turned back. She laughed. I laughed.

"How are you doing?" she called.

"Great! Great, thanks!" I put a lot of effort into sounding hearty and casual. I continued walking.

"See you later!"

"Right!"

I was thoroughly unnerved as I drove home, adrenalin pulsing through me, my hands shaky. It was crazy that such a brief encounter should have caused such upheaval, but there was no denying it. I had noticed her before, in the lounge. She was close to my own age, with expressive dark brown eyes and a smile that generated kilowatts. She was not conventionally beautiful, but attractive in ways beyond even her obvious charm and magnetism. Normally I would have thought there was a whiff of sex in my response, but that was impossible not just because she was a nun, but because I had not had anything even remotely resembling a sexual urge in more than two years. I couldn't remember what an erection felt like.

This is another salient feature of Hell: it's not sexy. Being damned is a full time job; and there is no time for, nor inclination to, sex.

Over the next few weeks, we chatted briefly as we crossed paths in the lounge. I made sure to note the times she was most likely to appear, since those few minutes were like a rush of oxygen in a life of suffocation.

One day she saw I was carrying a copy of a Buddhist scripture, The Diamond Sutra. It was one of the books I used to maintain some forlorn thread of connection to truths that were now dry as chalk dust. Though I could hardly bear to read it, her curiosity initiated a series of short, comparative religion discussions as we stood near the faculty mailboxes. The ideas we exchanged were incidental to the powerful energy that passed between us, the force that eventually led to much longer discussions.

We began meeting in the lounge at about four o'clock, when most everyone had left, and would talk until just before six, which was the convent dinner hour. We talked about a whole range of topics, but mostly about mysticism and food. I was fascinated to hear that her joining the convent had much more to do with her inner life than with any dedication to doctrinaire Catholicism. It also helped that she had an Italian mother, who had instilled in her and her siblings an appreciation of good food. In her company, I was temporarily permitted to love food again, to talk about it and dare to imagine enjoying it.

Along with elation, there came doubt and shame. I was afraid to reveal anything about my disastrous life. How could she not see all of it in my eyes, anyway? In my drooping shoulders? Though I wanted to hide from her, I felt renegade urges to unburden myself, too.

When I was not at school, I was a recluse. I would certainly never have allowed Ellen—or anyone else—into the ancient in-law bungalow I was renting in Chula Vista. It was as crusty and frozen-in-time as my landlady, Mrs. Stolp, a seventy-something widow with ramrod posture and a way of twitching her head that was distinctly avian. She let me know immediately that she did not like the idea of renting to a young single male. "Too much chance of misbehavin'." But I apparently looked lost and harmless enough to be acceptable. It didn't hurt that I would be teaching at a Catholic school, either, though she hastened to tell me she was not Catholic.

The place must have been built in the forties; its small windows allowed only a gloomy light even on the sunniest days. The bathroom was done in pink and pale green tile, the grout gone nearly black. Linoleum floors throughout. All the furnishings appeared to be original, in a style best described as "distressed colonial."

The mild climate in that part of the world must have been what created the thriving colony of black beetles that lived in the walls. They were like cockroaches, scores of them coming out at night, skittering across the kitchen floor. Sometimes the noise was so loud I felt moved to storm into the kitchen and kill a dozen of them with my shoe. It never seemed to slow them down much. I was forced to triple-wrap all my food that wasn't refrigerated.

It seemed appropriate that my little kitchen and dining area should become a kind of war zone, a reflection of my battle with food. Since I wouldn't allow myself to eat much, I unconsciously gravitated toward foods that were dense. Breakfast was often half a bagel with peanut butter, four or five dates, and tea. In the evening I refused to use a dinner plate, seeing them as an invitation to gluttony. My dinner had to fit on a salad plate, to keep portions small. I rarely ate potatoes. They were far too filling, and something I genuinely liked. I didn't eat desserts, either, for the same reasons. Lunch at school was always a small container of Alta-Dena yogurt, lemon or raspberry. Eating only yogurt in the middle of the school day was a satisfying deprivation, one that made afternoon classes an endurance test.

I took up running. I can't call it "jogging," because that word connotes something far more casual than my desperate attempts to exhaust myself. I ran every few days, when the tension in my body threatened to disable me. I usually ran at night, because I hated the idea of being observed, my spindly white legs in cutoff jeans, my ragged sweatshirt blousing in the wind. I ran in my neighborhood or sometimes around the field at school, after a talk with Ellen. Wherever I was, I ran like the berserker I had always been: until my chest was on fire, until I couldn't hear my feet hit the ground, until I saw stars.

In the morning, it was always exercise first. Pushups, jumping jacks, knee bends, sit ups. I was especially dedicated to sit ups because they were so difficult. Each time I raised my torso up, my tail bone would touch the floor and send a blast of flamethrower up my spine. There were often bloodstains on my boxers where my tailbone had been scraped raw. I made a short attempt at sitting meditation afterwards, maybe for ten minutes. I saw it as a charade, a Black Mass of contemplation. I accused myself of being superstitious, anxious to placate a god who didn't give a shit. The more scathing and violent the inner criticism, the more determined I was to sit and listen.

If anyone had questioned my relationship with Ellen, I would have been dumbfounded. It seemed so natural. She gave me C.S. Lewis books to read, and I gave her my copy of Ram Dass's *The Only Dance There Is*, complete with notations. She told me all about her family kitchen tradition of making ravioli from scratch, I told her about the wonderful *moelleux* Vouvrays from the 1930s and 40s I had tasted.

186

Ellen made my life at school bearable in ways beyond companionship, mostly by running interference with administrators and other teachers. If she happened to be with me when, for instance, four or five teachers were in the lounge, she artfully included me in the discussion, to the point where the others could easily mistake me for an animated, relaxed, normal human being. When I had an occasional meeting with the principal, I would find she had prepared the ground by collaring him earlier in the day, so that discussions of my inordinate number of detention-bound students or the size of my audio-visual budget were on a favorable trajectory and half-completed when I sat down.

In mid-November, after she cleared it with her Superior, we began a series of monthly dinners at the fanciest French restaurants in the area, nearly all in La Jolla and Del Mar. When at first she resisted the idea, citing the cost, I pleaded with her. I told her I had nothing to spend my paycheck on anyway, and this would provide me with great pleasure. This, though "pleasure" was an alien word that felt false and clumsy as it came from my lips. Was it about the pleasure of her company? Certainly. But it also might have been the pleasure of eating more and better food than I would ever have allowed myself when alone. Echoes of being with my sister at The Good Earth in Palo Alto.

We were self-conscious at first: a young nun in full regalia sitting in a swank restaurant, accompanied by a fellow as uncomfortable in his skin as he was in his old blue blazer and club tie. I was on edge, constantly afraid I might forget to lean forward as I sat, protecting my fiery tailbone from contact with the seat.

Ellen seemed to notice none of the strain in my manner. She acknowledged me, engaged me, seemingly untouched by my sickness. It was like being forgiven.

During that first dinner, she destroyed what remained of my well-established image of nuns, which admittedly had not been updated since grammar school. It wasn't her confessing to minor deviations from Church teachings—that, I expected—but when she said things like "I don't do Hell, and I don't do guilt," well, I couldn't help being thrilled and scandalized. Her unruffled audacity made me dizzy. I felt a spark of trust spring up in me, trust great enough that I needed only a few glasses of wine to begin telling her my story. It was the first time I recounted it to anyone.

I was cautious at first, worried that it would sound out-and-out insane, or that even a condensed version might bore her. I was aware only later that the tone I took in speaking was one of mild, humorous contempt, belittling myself in a doomed attempt to get some distance from the pain.

She was sympathetic in a way that bore no trace of phony sentiment. She asked a few questions, but was clear that such ineffable events should be the subject of respectful attention rather than judgment. When I saw she was not budging in her acceptance of me, I was shocked into a new realization: affectionate gratitude was quickly morphing into an attachment as deep as it was hopeless.

26.

Sister Ellen and I never spoke of our powerful attraction for each other, and rarely had physical contact. When we did touch—she grabbing my shoulder in frustration after one of my attempts at humor, I clutching her forearm to emphasize a discussion point—it was an electro-magnetic event. I reveled in the terrible tension, strong enough to nudge my attention away from Hell, ever so slightly. It was a different, easier kind of pain.

The situation reached a peak one night in early spring, when we had just finished dinner at a restaurant near the beach at Del Mar. It was unusually warm, the air soft and tropical, so we decided to take a walk. Once down on the sand, feeling the warm breeze, seeing the brilliant stars in their jewelry display and hearing the sleepy sound of the waves, we looked at each other and began to giggle. It became guffaws, belly laughs, barely-able-to-stand laughs. We'd had a lot of wine.

I fought to catch my breath. "Now this…is too perfect! Can you believe it?"

She fought to squeak out her words. "This is an

exact imitation of a date! But without the…stuff! The subtext! No muss, no fuss!"

"Hey, you've got an excuse, Sister; but what kind of kinky freak does this make me? The ultimate perversion!"

"You're managing it, though! You've got a handle on this! I think you're doing great!"

But the truth was, I wasn't doing great. I was probably listening too hard, but I felt suddenly forced by her words to abandon any thought of her going over the wall. The thin possibility of it was too nourishing—titillating?—to surrender easily. On the other hand, how could I ever speak up and risk such potentially devastating rejection? And, more serious still, how could I even consider saddling her with such a relationship? Sleep deprived, with an eating disorder, a haunted mind, and a nervous system about to crater, it was all I could do to make it from day to day. I could offer her nothing but a deep dive into my shame, a supporting role in the story of Hell. As it was, I was safe in my doom.

Ellen steadily expanded her role as my tireless advocate at school, not just with faculty and administrators, but with students, too. In many ways, the students were a tougher sell. They had to deal with a young, obviously inexperienced teacher who expected them to be attentive and interested in learning, and at the same time to somehow acknowledge his strange internal battle, even as he put tremendous effort into trying to hide it. He was obviously not enjoying his job.

I could just imagine Ellen talking to students about me.

Ellen: "Oh, Mr. Moser read that book. We had an interesting discussion; you should ask him about it."

Student: "Uh, well, I don't really know Mr. Moser, and he seems a little up-tight. I mean, he's so nervous, and kind of grim all the time."

Ellen: "No, no, he's a great guy! Really! He can be a little shy at first, but go and talk to him. He'll be glad to do it. No kidding!"

Student: "Um, okay. Sure. I'll do that…sometime."

Not long after our walk on the beach, I drove her up to Malibu to have dinner with my parents. As a weekend outing, it was unusual to say the least, but it had its own logic. The main objective was of course to allow me more time with Ellen, but I reasoned that it would also be interesting for my parents to encounter a new, young face of Catholicism, one that I was certain would shock them a little, but delight them, too. Though I had seen them only once since the departure of the Ecstasy, at that time they had been touchingly sweet and solicitous, understanding that something terrible had happened, yet not asking difficult questions. They helped me believe that my shame might not be glaringly visible to the rest of the world.

As expected, Ellen charmed them thoroughly. My mother had an extra martini before dinner, I noticed, and had a disconcerting, mischievous twinkle in her eye all evening. She was practically winking at me. My father, free of alcohol for nearly four years, was unusually reserved. The headline Small World moment came in discovering that Ellen's father and my mother had been close friends at Balboa High in San Francisco, circa

1942. My parents' astonishment was total, Ellen's and mine less so. The discovery seemed of a piece with our short but extraordinary history.

On the drive back, she floated the outrageous idea of having me direct the school's spring musical. I was horrified. It was true I had agreed to teach a Speech and Drama class that semester, on the strength of some dabbling in theater at Stanford, but the thought of taking on such a huge responsibility pushed me into a cold sweat. It is hard to say why I eventually agreed to do it. What is certain is that the administration agreed only because Ellen accepted the position of Assistant Director, where she could do most of the heavy lifting in enlisting parents and faculty to fill key positions—something I could never have done.

We now spent our after-hours discussion time talking not about mysticism and Francis of Assisi, but about timelines and details of the show, which was to be *My Fair Lady*. It was all very disturbing and destabilizing. I was spooked by my surge of genuine interest in it, and tried my best to keep some emotional distance. Could I let this superficial "extra-curricular activity" occupy the empty space I was holding for the return of the ecstatic state? My internal narrator treated the show like a tedious chore—it was a high school musical, for God's sake. I wanted to look at it in the same way I looked at teaching itself: a sad, meaningless, consolation-prize of busy work, like digging a hole and filling it up again. Like eating another bowl of tasteless gruel. Despite myself, I couldn't deny the spark of interest that had been struck.

With rehearsals four nights a week, I was having a hard time keeping up with my lesson plans, and I stopped my evening running. What was unusual was the amount of sympathy my students showed me. With little grumbling, they accepted writing assignments or workbook exercises that lasted the entire period. They had lots of questions about how things were going, and whether we would be ready for opening night. I looked out at them and realized that many of them had been waiting for something like this, a situation where I would show some need, some vulnerability, and would ask for their help. Though still far too certain of my wasted and shameful life to articulate it, I knew somewhere in me that I had been waiting for that moment, too.

Rehearsal schedule also affected after-school discussions with Ellen. Refusing to pre-empt them, we instead pushed them further into the evening. Never starting much before 9:30, we often talked until midnight or even 1 a.m., which left us constantly exhausted. It also created a pretty healthy scandal.

One morning after a particularly late discussion—about the meaning of "sin," ironically enough—Ellen did not appear in the teachers' lounge as usual. Only at lunch time did I find her there. I knew something is wrong. She was trying to be casual, and Ellen never *tried* to be anything. Eying the eight or ten other teachers in the lounge, she said she would see me at rehearsal.

That night, she told me what I already knew: it was about our late-night talks. Her Superior had had a word with her, just a friendly warning. Not that anything was wrong. But spending too much time with a young, single male teacher could give an unfortunate impression. We didn't want tongues wagging, though of course things are completely above board. Etcetera.

Over tea at ten o'clock, we laughed about the whole adventure. I mean *honestly*. The idea of Ellen and I in some illicit affair was hilarious. We agreed that our discussions would now end at 11:30, no exceptions. We would even limit them to three nights a week. Our resolutions did not last.

At home late that night, bitterness caught up with me. That the one ray of light in my life should be cause for public criticism was more than I could bear. As I lay on my bed, wide awake, my anger and frustration easily overriding my exhaustion, I cursed my life in the most vicious terms.

It was now more than two years ago and the truth is, I can't remember exactly what waking up on that winter morning in 1975 was like. It might have been like being born or dying. One second you're on one side of the threshold, the next you're on the other; and for an eyelash of time, you are not sure where you are. Freshly departed, recently arrived, not yet out of the shadow of the doorway. But if the Great Intelligence of the universe was on both sides of the door, what difference could the passage make? What did I imagine I had lost when I sat up with a gasp, in bed that morning? What was I hoping to find by stumbling into the living room, then falling to the floor in the most desperate supplication? I thought it might be another test, just a temporary dry spell, a small version of the reversals of fortune experienced by Job. You know: Those sores on your body are terribly painful, and it was hard to see your children die, sure, but keep the faith! It will all be restored to you eventually, and then we'll have a hell of a party. You're my main man! You didn't think I would just fuck you over and leave you to rot?

Or was I like Abraham, being asked to give up that son who meant the world to him. Go through that door, sacrifice your Ecstasy on that altar. The angel you see here on my right is standing by with a knife, for your convenience.

But, but, but. But my body had been so loose-limbed and blessedly relaxed. On my back, unmoving through the night, with deep, slow, almost imperceptible breath. Why not leave well enough alone, why not allow me more days, months, and years in that state? To Your greater glory? So that I might cleave more closely to Thy Divine Will? Not my will, but Thy Will be done?

Even as reverent words bounced around in my head, down in that wordless, thoughtless blood pudding of my dark heart there was the anger that, given voice, would have said, "I will accept Thy Will, of course, even if it means You desire one of Your most faithful servants to live in this shithole You have consigned him to; but I will not give You the divine satisfaction of seeing me bolt from the flock and give up my dedication to Love, Truth, and Beauty—even if these words never again have any reality for me. I will climb up on that altar myself, draw the knife across some tastefully vulnerable part of my body—no pulsing fountains, no geysers of blood— and die as some sort of sacrifice, perhaps even one not at all pleasing in Your eyes.

It might be a very slow death. Blood seeping out of my body over, say, thirty or forty or even fifty years.

27.

The show came off better than I could have hoped. On closing night, I stood in the wings struggling to identify the strange feeling that coursed through me like a drug. That? Oh, right. *Satisfaction.* It was so unfamiliar that I might have reflexively buried it, remained cool and hopeless and unfazed, had it not been for its overwhelming evidence all around me.

Without my knowing it, Ellen had arranged for the little choir of maids who sang the "Congratulations" to Professor Higgins after his triumphant presentation of Eliza at the ball, to come onstage and sing "Congratulations, Mr. Moser, for your glorious victory." A sustained wave of applause forced me out of the wings. I had warned everyone against doing this sort of thing; I had specified that I did not want a lot of windy speeches from parents and teachers at the end. I wanted a *professional* feel to the show. Crisp, well-paced, full of assurance. Why I said this is mysterious. I appeared to have been ignoring the fact that it was indeed a high school musical, a project realized by a community that very much wanted to acknowledge those who created it.

But at that moment I was feeling testy. Curtly, I announced that there were too many people who worked too hard for me to mention them all. I thanked everyone for supporting us and coming to the show in such great numbers. I walked off. Though I could feel the dismay of everyone around me, I was listening only to the familiar, withering voice in my head: "It is, after all, just a high school musical, isn't it? Is it the reason for your life? It matters not a whit in the grand scheme of things."

At the cast and crew party that followed, I was approached by several faculty members who praised the show, but also gingerly questioned my decision not to recognize the various parents and teachers who were key to its success. While internally despising these people, I thanked them and allowed that, yes, well, that might have been a good idea. Too late now. Sorry.

At 2 a.m., when I arrived home, those teachers' faces were still in front of me, their words dogging me. I saw that, even giving me the benefit of the doubt, they were genuinely concerned at my strange inability to give and accept praise, to be enthusiastic about what the students had achieved. Nobody had asked me to die for the world's sins; they just wanted me to show appreciation and kindness to co-workers and students. And, at the end of more than six years of earnest seeking for freedom and truth and understanding, apparently I couldn't do even that much.

It was hard to look at.

But for some reason I also saw that this was not another occasion to pummel myself with criticism. That had become a pretty murderous tape loop, and it needed my attention. In a way, it needed affection, too—something I had so little of. I could feel something giving way in me, though it was barely perceptibly and distinctly un-miraculous. Now, instead of an endless, dark, narrow corridor, there was the outline of a landscape in front of me. It had intriguing and varied features; it was inviting me to explore it a little, to go this way instead of that, or maybe some other way altogether. Not because to do so would be right or wrong, but because it would be *interesting*. Though this view was at that moment too alien and threatening to acknowledge wholeheartedly, I was never again able completely to ignore the chance that something seemingly random thrown in my path might be nothing more than valuable experience, and not a confirmation of my damnation. It was the bare possibility of a possibility, but it was something.

Showering one morning about a week later, I came face to face with the fact that there was another school year out there waiting for me after a few months of vacation. The huge workload, the energy needed to control the classroom, the obligation to supervise extra-curricular activities. And of course the ridiculously small paychecks. It was just another in my world of despondent thoughts until I realized that there was something I could do about it. No one was forcing me to do this job. There was no gun to my head. It was obvious that I should quit.

I didn't catch up with Sister Ellen until after school, when the teachers' lounge was mercifully empty. I blurted out the news. She showed no surprise, but instead gave me a resigned, rueful smile.

"Sister, this is the right thing to do!"

She scrunched up her face and said, "I know! I know it is!"

"You know how I know it's right? Because I still feel good about it even when I think about paying back student loans, even when I admit that the loan officer was right in hesitating to give me the money. Now *that's* powerful."

"Do you know what you're going to do? Go to Ojai?"

I had often spoken of Alan Hooker and Ojai, and had told her about his periodic phone calls which included mention of how the restaurant wine list could use updating, and that I was always welcome there. "Could be. I can always work in a wine shop if I have to. I don't much care."

I looked at my great friend with all the affection my haunted self would allow. I marveled at her honest, direct gaze; her playfulness; her huge generosity toward me and everyone else. How had this miraculous friend materialized? It didn't matter. I was just deeply grateful.

Over our last dinner a few weeks later, we agreed to stay in touch however we could. And we have held to that agreement, over a period of more than forty years. Before I left San Diego, I made a point of telling her my lone cosmic certainty: if there was a God, Sister Ellen was one of the proofs of Her existence.

I suppose I fully expected to end up in Ojai, working at the Ranch House. The surprise was that the experience should turn out to be a far subtler view of Hell than what I had known in San Diego. During my year of teaching, there had been a direct correlation between my constant feelings of dread and the activities I was engaged in: mollifying the administration, desperately trying to appear "normal" to my fellow faculty members, but most of all coping with unruly students. It was Hell in its identifiable, user-friendly form. The old-fashioned Hell. The reason I continued doing it for so long was exactly *because* it was so terrible. I was comfortable.

But now there was Ojai.

Though I stubbornly asserted my independence by insisting I not live with them when I first arrived in town, Alan and Helen took me to the restaurant every day it was open. For weeks, Wednesday through Sunday, we sat at table number 10 at 6 o'clock and had dinner. It was there I was blindsided by this new and exotic Hell. I had no defense against it. I would sit down and Alan would ask, "How about an aperitif? Does a Kir Royale sound good? A glass of good Chablis? Would that suit you?"

How to deal with this? A relentless parade of delicious foods, whatever I might want, served by wonderfully friendly people in one of the most beautiful garden settings I had ever seen. On Sundays, there was flute and harpsichord music. How about some Scottish smoked salmon, with capers, sieved egg, and Bermuda onion? And then maybe some broiled swordfish with a buttery Bercy sauce—oh, and let's have a bottle of Francois Jobard's 1973 Meursault with that, yes? Of course we want to hear about dessert!

I gained weight, a rare form of pain. The more lavishly I was treated, the more I felt like running out of the restaurant screaming. It was not just that I felt monstrously guilty, unworthy of this treatment, but in the few scattered moments I might have come to terms with all that, I would then have to rein in my fear that all this luxury was put in my path to distract me from the ascetic destiny that was really mine. It was diabolical temptation, and Alan was Mephistopheles. It was a test. Do you want that cup of tea? Don't take it. That's fine. But if you're passing on the tea, how about a glass of Vosne-Romanée from Jean Grivot?

Hotels in Ojai were pricey, and there were no rentals—at least nothing a prematurely retired teacher could afford. My old college friend Dan Moynier had recently moved back to Ojai from Santa Barbara, and was now working at the Ranch House alongside a day job in real estate. He found me a vacant tract house where I could stay for free while the absentee owners decided what to do with it.

The place was vintage 1950s, with a brown, dead lawn and a few brave junipers still clinging to life in the beds along the front. Inside it was all nut-brown carpeting and stark white walls. The stripped-down kitchen was without stove or refrigerator. There was no gas service or electricity, which meant no light beyond my flashlight. Because the water was still connected, however, I was able to take cold showers.

In so many ways, it was custom-designed for me. Though Alan pointed out many times at dinner that I would be much more comfortable at their house, and that I could pay a little rent if it eased my mind, I refused. He said, as he would so often when confronted with my stubbornness, "Suit yourself." It was only later that I drove him to exclaim, "My God, but you're willful!"

During the day there was nothing I needed to do, and I saw no one. It was monotonously beautiful and hot. I woke up early, usually around five, my heart beating furiously, adrenalin by the quart in my system, my tailbone fiery. I immediately put on shorts and a T-shirt and went running. It was much like what I had done in San Diego, except that the surroundings were far more beautiful, and I ran much farther, often six or seven miles. Even in the relative cool of the morning, the air smelled scorched, like hot granite, a smell that mingled with the perfume of lemon and orange groves and the spicy smell of dry sagebrush. The groves seemed endless, stretching to the foot of the mountains that formed the narrow valley that sheltered the little town of Ojai.

I sometimes panicked, realizing that my relentless, ungovernable drive would not let me slow down or stop until I reached the house, so there was always the risk that my legs would give way and I would fall. On my return, feeling towering rage at nothing in particular, I would run right up to the front door of the house, and, like an exhausted boxer gamely snorting and jabbing at the air after fourteen rounds, I would tersely assure myself even before I stopped that I could run still farther if I wanted to.

The first Friday night after my arrival, I put on my bright blue double-knit flares and one of my permanent press ivory shirts with the hopelessly wrinkled cuffs, and drove to the restaurant to begin my work life in Ojai.

It turned out I was a pretty good sommelier. It might have been because there was just the right amount of performing involved, or because I really did love talking about the different wines, trying to describe them. But I think the real reason I was good at it was my great gratitude at having something immediate and demanding to do, something that didn't allow for a lot of introspection. You show up at the table, greet the guests and ask if anyone would like an aperitif. You get the order. You prepare it, you bring it to the table. You're done.

By contrast, as a teacher I had a million choices in preparing a lesson plan, and I was always sure I'd made a hash of it. And I was unhappy dealing with that certain percentage of students who were institutionally bound to play the adversary, to assert themselves by violating the rules of which I was the embodiment. At the restaurant, the people I interacted with were—gasp!—*happy* to be there, and not displeased to see me, an agent of their enjoyment. They weren't acting out to impress their peer group. They weren't wondering why they were there in the first place. Wait a minute: they were just there to have *dinner*! That this minor subsection of the social contract could be so much simpler than teaching was a thrillingly obvious realization for me. It confirmed the idea that I was ill-suited to teaching, and that it had been totally sensible to quit. For once, my intuition had outrun my mind and I had actually done the right thing. I hadn't sought advice from anyone, hadn't drawn up a list of pros and cons, hadn't lost sleep over it.

When service ended on that Friday night around 11 o'clock, and I was given a beautiful plate of broiled salmon and fresh steamed vegetables, I felt more guilt. How could I possibly deserve such beautiful food? And wasn't it just an obstacle on the road to Freedom? Wasn't I selling my birthright for an admittedly delicious mess of pottage? But beyond all that was something new: the creeping, subversive suspicion that it might be appropriate for me to be in Ojai, working at the restaurant, doing just what I was doing. I knew that much of my justification for being there had to do with Alan—who he was, what he was about, what I might learn from him.

28.

To no one's surprise, after a few more weeks I moved in with Alan and Helen. My campsite home had been sold, and workers were due to start remodeling. When I had stowed my boxes in the garage and put my few clothes in my new room, which also doubled as an office, I sat down in the living room with Alan to have a business discussion. I told him I wanted to pay rent, and something for food. He said they got almost all their food from the restaurant, but that I could pay fifteen dollars a month rent if that was what I wanted. I said that wasn't much. He said it was a very small room.

I was nervous. "But what am I *doing* here, Alan? What is it about?"

"Please. Please, my friend. Try not to fuss about this. There is no point in chewing on it, trying to explain everything. Just do this for now. It's your nature to want to know everything, but just let this alone for a while."

"But how will I know when I'm supposed to leave?"

He sat back in his chair, a gentle smile on his face.

"Oh, don't worry about that. When the time comes, you'll know. Believe me. You'll know."

So began a period of a little more than two years at Alan and Helen's. I was very uncomfortable at first, of course. It was one thing to stop over for a night at the house, a break in the action of a busy life that existed elsewhere. It was another to reside in that space, in that small room with three watercolors of Paris Alan had put up to make me feel "at home," with the sound of the little fountain in the backyard goldfish pond coming in my window at night, musical but somehow lonely, too. At age twenty-eight, I couldn't tell anyone about my big career plans. I had no credentials to flash, no names to drop.

When I got into bed (an actual bed!) that first night, I was certain I would wake up early. I was too nervous and self-conscious to sleep well, so it would be no trouble making it to breakfast. Waking up the next morning after a heavy, exhausted sleep, I grabbed my watch from the nightstand. Almost eight-thirty. I was mortified. Either they would indulge me or they would criticize. Either way, it would be unbearable. And on my first morning as a semi-permanent boarder, no less. I was prepared to apologize for my own existence. I cursed myself as I pulled on my pants and a shirt and staggered out to the table.

I found Alan as he had been on my previous visits, wrapped in a beautiful robe, sitting at his end of the table, reading the LA Times. Helen was standing at the stove, stirring her millet cereal. At their places and at mine was a beautiful plate with a half-papaya on it, and sliced strawberries in its scooped-out cavity. There were mismatched but equally beautiful cups and saucers, butter, several unmarked jars of jam, and a large basket of breads which I recognized as coming from the restaurant: whole wheat, soy sesame, rye, and oatmeal. To Alan's left, on a rolling cart, a toaster oven and a large teapot with a thick, knitted cozy on it.

Looking up placidly, Alan smiled. "Well, sir, I do hope you slept. A good night's sleep makes such a difference."

Helen said, "Well you can say that again. Sit thee down, my dear."

"I'm really sorry to have held things up. I was hoping you would have just gone ahead." I felt pitiful, and sounded like it.

Alan put the paper to one side, raised his eyebrows and smiled. "Not at all. There seems to be no rush whatsoever. None that I can find, anyway. Tea?"

I quickly learned the unspoken household rule: Eating together was important. It was a priority, a vital connection, a kind of secular sacrament. It mystified me at first, having been raised in a family that rarely ate together, and where meals were either 15-minute interludes on the way to something else, or a half-conscious accompaniment for television shows like *Bonanza* or *Have Gun Will Travel*. Life was about velocity so ferocious that it tended to blur actual discrete experiences. It wasn't evil or depraved—it was just the way it was in Los Angeles in the late fifties and early sixties. Imaginations were routinely starved; children absorbed bad juju. It was the banality of banality.

My sister and I ate sitting on stools in the kitchen, on opposite sides of an oversized, pull-out cutting board.

Cooking held no fascination for my mother, and she made no secret of her resentment at having to prepare a meal for us at 6 p.m., and another one for my father when he came home at 8:30 or so. I had occasion to wonder: when did my mother eat? And: why did my father come home so late? Had I been a little older and more world-wise, I might have answered these questions more easily.

My father was not in a good mood when he came home in the evening. We knew to stay out of his way and turn the channel to a boring *NBC White Paper Report*, or *Armstrong Circle Theater*, or whatever. He would drink two or three tall scotches and then have a TV tray of food put before him. Woe to all of us if it was not to his liking. In those moments an icy tension would grip the house. My parents' clashes were rarely loud; most often they were silent standoffs that left the air full of dangerous vapors.

To be affluent at that time didn't mean you used your resources to buy the best, freshest foods available. In LA, having some money meant you bought the coolest food toys, the latest trends. The frozen beef stroganoff—with its own special sauce packet! The cheddar cheese in a can, the frozen pastrami sandwich in a convenient foil pouch for reheating. It was the dawn of Lucky Charms. I consumed a lot of these items lying on the sofa, paper towel heaped with goodies perched on my chest. Or I just ate standing up, in front of the fridge with the door open.

It was all I had known, so this new Ojai model of eating would normally have caused me to squirm. It was only my complete psychological exhaustion that led me to accept it. For many months, I was like an infant who didn't have even a small spark of the Terrible Twos in him, no ability to refuse even the most minor request or suggestion. On a night the restaurant was closed, Alan might say to me, "I'm thinking about making a fresh veggie frittata. Does that sound good?" And I would mutter "Fine with me," both of us knowing he could have suggested a domestic pet soufflé and my response would have been the same.

There was another revelation that came alive for me at Alan and Helen's, too: Beautiful Things Matter. Before arriving in Ojai, I had paid little attention to the hardware involved in consuming a meal—the plates, the cups, the flatware. As a child, these trappings were either unremarkable, or deserving of attention primarily because they were expensive. No adult had ever communicated to me an actual gut-level, personal admiration of the beauty of any tableware. No one had ever picked up a tea cup and commented appreciatively on its qualities. But now I was fascinated by the beauty of Wedgewood's Katani Crane, or Spode's The Queen's Bird. There were artisanal ceramic honey jars from Germany, too. There were graceful-looking wooden toast tongs from Carmel, hand-painted tile hot plates from England. Having all these on the table was its own kind of feast.

Alan and I quickly cemented our habit of talking after breakfast for two or three hours. For many months it was hard for me to sit there, not just because of the terrible burning at the base of my spine, but because I didn't fully trust him. He didn't look the part of the wise man, the teacher. The image of Pir Vilayat was still very much with me as a prime example of the real thing: gray beard, flowing robes, leader of an esoteric tradition. By contrast, here was a jolly, red-cheeked restaurateur who lived with his wife in a tract house in Ojai. My mind played games with me. Of course Alan said some interesting things. No doubt about it. But what if…just what if my being there was a Test to see if I was ready for a still more high-powered teacher? What if Alan had been placed in my path to suck me into a sensual, materialistic swamp of wine and food, so that I would never do whatever it was I needed to do to regain the ecstatic state? I was so delusional that initially I even spent time considering the notion that I was somehow "more advanced" than Alan, and that *I* was there to teach *him*. As if all of this were some kind of martial arts display, and I was demanding to see the color of his belt. It was deeply confusing. I mean, one minute he was saying mysterious and profound things, and the next he was just a nice old guy who had a res-taurant. What did it mean?

Things didn't get simpler when I discovered that Alan was gay, or at least bi-sexual. I think Dan Moynier gave me the news, actually just confirming my suspi-cions. His and Helen's separate bedrooms suddenly made sense, and his extra-boyish manner and taste in silk bathrobes fit in, too. I was disturbed and paranoid at first. So *this* was what Alan was really about. After all, who wouldn't notice the steady stream of young people from the restaurant staff—overwhelmingly men like Dan and me—coming to the house day after day. Was I set up to be some kind of cultish bum boy for this man? Here I was in a living situation that in my mind held out some hope of getting me back to the Ecstasy, and now I had to deal with the idea that the whole thing might be about something else—something pretty sordid.

Upset as I was, somewhere deep inside I knew the whole issue was a red herring. For a man nearly thirty to be living in the home of friends old enough to be his grandparents, and working four days a week at their restaurant—well, that was outlandish enough. What difference if one of them turned out to be gay? Gay was neither here nor there. It was irrelevant. My intuition, of which historically I seem to have had practically none, said yes to being there, in the face of all of it. I knew I was there to benefit in ways that were thankfully hidden from me.

The following day Alan brought up the topic, saying Dan had told him about his conversation with me. He said he had been aware of his sexual orientation since he was a teenager, and that it had been a burden until he joined the Theosophical Lodge in Columbus. After that, his teacher became his decision-maker.

I couldn't restrain myself from blurting out the question that was burning me: "You mean you not only got *married* because Mrs. Bollenbacher told you to, but *knowing* you were homosexual, on top of it?"

"My dear friend," he said, "as I told you, this is bound to be something very difficult for you to understand. Jenny Bollenbacher was my Teacher, and I accepted her insight without question. You must certainly be aware that every day people make ruinous decisions based on their 'free will,' decisions that benefit them far less than my marriage to Helen."

"But what about Helen? She must have known about this! How could she do it?"

He chuckled. "Well, you'll have to ask her about that. But her view of Jenny was not very different from mine. What might help you to understand would be to think of how it was with the Sufi fellow—what was his name?"

"Pir Vilayat Khan." I had already told Alan a little bit about my time with the Sufis and about Pir Vilayat, though it would take more time for the full story to come out. "So it was like that?"

"I expect so. You establish a very deep trust with the Teacher, not related to anything they say, necessarily. There is a rooted connection on a level that is untouchable. This man didn't ask you to do anything in particular, did he? But he might well have. What would you have done then?"

"Good question. If Pir Vilayat had asked me to eat one vegetarian meal a day, stand on my head for an hour and sing the Names of God, I'd have done it, no question. But I don't think I would have jumped off the Golden Gate Bridge if he'd asked me to."

"And a good thing, too!" Alan laughed his belly laugh. "I have to say, I didn't look at marrying Helen as the equivalent of jumping off a bridge! We had a normal sex life for years, but we both recognized long ago that our relationship was about exploring consciousness, each in our own way."

The conversation was good for me. It removed the chance of there being an unspoken, festering subtext not just in our discussions, but in our relationship as a whole. I admit I was a little touchy for a while after that. At breakfast one morning, in the middle of our discussion, Alan reached out and took hold of my forearm to make a point. With all my youthful insecurity on display, I said, "Alan, I really would prefer you didn't do that." He raised his eyebrows, nodded and said, "Fair enough."

29.

It wasn't long before I recounted to Alan the details of my experiences in heaven and hell. To him, it was confirmation of what he already knew. To me, it was a huge unburdening, a confession. He listened carefully, not speaking much as I filled out the picture over several days. I remember being shocked into temporary silence near the beginning of my story, when out of the blue he looked at me with a gentle, querulous expression and said, "Don't you think it's extraordinary that I like you more than you like yourself?"

I recounted most everything, from severe fasting to seminars with Pir Vilayat, from the explosion in my chest that knocked me down to the morning when it all disappeared and the horror began. I didn't spare him any of my frustration and rage. I demanded answers.

"Why should all of this happen, Alan? What could be the point? It wasn't that I had any bad intentions. I was just taking a cue from the purple book: when you work on yourself, ultimately that work benefits everyone."

He set the edge of his flattened hand perpendicular

to the table, and moved it up and down. "The curtain has to come down on the first act before it can come up on the second."

"But what if you've had the denouement and the finale in the first act? Where can I go from here? Because, really and truly, *that* – whatever it was—was all I could ever hope for. How do you get beyond a connection, a state like that?"

"My dear friend, forgive me, but no matter what you do…*you*…cannot know God."

I was irritated. Oh yeah? I thought. You weren't there. But what I said was: "Maybe not, Alan. But as far as I'm concerned, there isn't anything else that's particularly worth doing. What am I supposed to do? Go to school? Give swimming lessons? Get a doctorate? Join the circus? It all looks pretty ridiculous. So if, according to you, I am launched on a hopeless mission, then so be it. Make the most of it." I was leaning toward him, speaking tersely.

He looked at me with astonishment, then smiled faintly as he shook his head. "My God, but you're willful." The refrain I would hear so many times.

My ceaseless hammering, my constant "why?" drew another answer from him one day about a week later. I was in a sullen mood, having lived in the house long enough to be comfortable in displaying something other than a pained social smile. Alan didn't seem to notice. He was animated as he said, "You must realize how this unfolds. First, there is the romance and the honeymoon—champagne and flowers. Great euphoria. But then what's next? It's the hard work of building a life, your relationship with life. Now, instead of all manner of gifts, what you get is: 'Did you remember to call the plumber?' and "What are we having for dinner?" It's a necessary, crucial part of the work of life, the great work, the Magnum Opus."

Through the flames of my indignation, I realized dimly then that no answer Alan could offer would be enough. There would likely be no magic incantation that would transform my world in an instant. I was desolate, yes, but oh, so unbowed.

I drifted further into hopelessness. Often after our talks, I would go into my room, sit down in the swivel desk chair, and stay there for an hour or so, with a terrible headache. It felt as if hot nails were being driven into my medulla. I couldn't move, couldn't think. It was completely debilitating, not to mention frightening. In my own perception I was so innocent of wrongdoing that all the pain made me even more self-righteous and furious.

Alan knew I was at my limit, and one morning came into my room as I sat. He nodded grimly and said, "I can see the little man there inside you. Sitting cross-legged, eyes closed." He raised his chin, looking very serious and determined. "Nothing will distract him from his dedication to his vows. Nothing. No matter what happens, he's going to ignore it. He'd rather *die* than give up. He's impervious to...*everything*."

Sitting there, frozen with pain, I barely heard him.

Late one afternoon in the spring of 1979, I came home from a visit to the health food store in town with some news: there would be a three-day weekend seminar with Pir Vilayat Khan at a state park near Santa Barbara.

Alan raised his eyebrows. "Sounds like it might be interesting for you. Are you thinking of going?"

I was indignant. "Absolutely *not*!"

"So you don't think it might be a good thing? Get right to the heart of things and see what issues you left behind?"

"Alan, I just don't think it's honest—or sane—to go to that thing like some kind of undercover agent. My whole experience with him was very confusing, and like I told you, I might never know what it was about. But I'm sure what he's doing isn't some sort of 'Jonestown' manipulation at all. It's just a human truth that if someone walks up to you, taps you on the forehead and you see stars or throw up or whatever, you are likely to follow them around."

Alan shook his head. "Now please don't misunderstand me here. I am not suggesting that you attend this weekend as some sort of mole or turncoat. But this is an opportunity to *look* at what responses the experience pulls out of you. The more open and honest you can be, the better. Surely this man would be in favor of that."

I couldn't believe I was hearing this from the man who so fiercely rejected gurus and teachers. "Do you truly think I should go? I should give them my sixty dollars? It's two nights! And I know what it'll be like: peanut butter for lunch and brown rice for dinner, basically."

He laughed. "No Premier Cru Burgundies over there, that's the truth. But would that really stop you?"

Now I couldn't believe what *I* was saying. "You're probably right. Unbelievable that I would even *think* of doing this. But it probably is the right thing to do."

"My dear friend, it's no use if it's right for me. It has to be right for you."

On a Friday night in early May, I drove over to Santa Barbara.

Naturally, I was entertaining that monotonous little voice in me, quietly suggesting that this event might just be the one to open the gates to the ecstatic state again. Something would happen during the chanting, or during a meditation. Or Pir Vilayat would catch my eye during one of his talks, sparks would fly, I would go out of myself and have to be brought back to consciousness by the kind ministrations of people around me.

My unacknowledged fantasy was a version of the Prodigal Son story. To be embraced and accepted after all my mad wanderings and self-destructive decisions. To sit in a circle quietly with Pir Vilayat, Krishnamurti, and Alan, proving definitively that "It," the Truth, the object of my search, was the same for all, differing only in its description.

My actual experience of the retreat showed me just how alienated I was from the Sufi world. I was more than ever an outsider there, outnumbered and outgunned. The people around me had their connections with each other, their Sufi names, Sufi songs, Sufi dances; I had my pride, a job at a restaurant, and the crippling pain of the previous four years. Bitter defensiveness kicked in. What gave it extra sting was the realization that I had begun using the Alan/Krishnamurti axis as a kind of weapon against the activities of the retreat. It became "us against them." Whether religion was a blessing or a plague, whether Pir Vilayat was a powerful mystic or a mountebank—no exploration of those questions or any others could unfold because I was so spectacularly threatened.

Just seeing Pir Vilayat felt like a reproach. As always, he oozed nobility, gentleness, and heart. I still had no idea who he was, but I knew who I was: a terrified kid from LA who couldn't figure out which way was up.

I left the gathering after spending only one night in the small, open A-frame assigned to me. When on the second evening I heard there was to be a celebration of some sort, certainly including lots of singing and alleluias, I packed up my car and left without a word to anyone. I had nothing to celebrate, and could not bear the idea of pretending that I did.

30.

Back at the house, after a welcome shower, I sat down with Alan. He was watchful, unsmiling. Why did I launch into an animated defense of Pir Vilayat?

"I don't know who he is, Alan, but he's Somebody, with a capital 'S'. He's very powerful, and he uses that power to serve others. Just because I don't seem to have a connection to any of it now doesn't make it less real."

"Do you think this man can take away your guilt?"

"I doubt it. I wish he could, though."

"But if he could. Hypothetically, would you then become his follower again? Would your relief translate into gratitude, which becomes admiration, which becomes obedience? I am just suggesting this, now. No need to jump at it right away, accepting or rejecting. Just stay with the question. There is so much vitality, so much mystery in it!"

"Okayokayokay, I get it!" I was exasperated and sleep-deprived, and it was hard not to race to the end of it. "If he performed a miracle for me, like relieving my guilt—and that *would* be a miracle—I would probably be his follower, yeah. Is that the way it works? I become someone who needs him, then he needs me as a student? Then it's all a trap. I reinforce his role as a teacher, he reinforces mine as a student, and we are both stuck there forever?"

Alan was sitting upright in his chair, smiling broadly now. "I don't know. Find out!" As I started to speak, he raised his hand. "And for God's sake don't ask me *how* to do it!"

After lunch, I walked into my room and sat down at the desk. I took a sheet of paper from the drawer and began a letter to Pir Vilayat, requesting that he release me from my initiation into the Sufi community, and from my vows.

After writing a single line I stopped, with an unfamiliar question in front of me: What had actually happened then, nearly four years ago, in that house in San Anselmo? Unusual for me, I had taken the initiative and gone upstairs with the others who were taking vows. I hadn't talked about it beforehand with anyone at the gathering. I didn't consider that the other people up on that landing had probably confirmed the event with someone in the organization days or weeks in advance. I went upstairs only because I was so inebriated with love, swept away by the power and beauty of this teacher, and of existence. There was no question but that I should be initiated. And no one stopped me. None of the helpers asked what I was doing there. Someone opened the door to the room, and there he was. I sat on the straight-backed chair, knee-to-knee with him. He gave me some practices—to cultivate courage and open the heart—but then: he hadn't given me a Sufi name, as he had done with so many others. And why hadn't I recited vows of some kind? I had been oblivious to all of it because I was sure it was impossible to be so drunk with love and not be an initiate.

In this fresh light, there was no getting around it: I was not a member of the Sufi Order after all.

There was something else, too. Pir Vilayat had said more—oh so much more—during my encounter with him. Just before the interview ended, he looked at me deeply, unblinking, and said the words I could never forget. Just a handful of words, but ones that, when placed on the scales of a lifetime outweigh many millions of others, most of them so light that they drift off into space and are lost to all, with no loss to anyone. He said the blessed thing, the horrible thing, the thing I was bound to cling to, ferociously. He said: "If things go according to plan… you will have your heart's desire. Enlightenment."

Sitting at the desk, I realized how solemn had been my resolution to myself never to tell anyone about that moment. I hadn't even told Sister Ellen. At first I thought omitting that bit of the story was just an editorial choice. No need to go into all that, etc. But as I sat at the desk I knew it would be the one thing I could never bring myself to tell Alan, either.

Instinctively, I protected it, feeling it was sacred. Telling anyone—much less writing it down in a memoir—would be some kind of cosmic betrayal, smashing a priceless vessel that was in my safekeeping. More to the point, telling anyone might prevent it from happening; but I wasn't so keen to explain it that way.

I was afraid of losing something I never had—*could* never have—and knew nothing about.

I wrote my letter to Pir Vilayat anyway that day. I asked to be released from any vows or commitments I might have made to the Sufi Order of the West, so that I might get on with the work at hand, whatever it might be. I said, "I bear no rancor toward the Sufi order, much less toward you and your work. If my experience with the Order inadvertently created a guilt-ridden, monstrous, delusional fantasy, then let this letter be the occasion to destroy it. If, alternately, by this letter I am abandoning some crucial position I was supposed to occupy, if I am failing miserably at some vital task I can't quite identify, if I am cursed and damned to outer darkness, well then, I'll catch up with you on the next round, in a future eon or in some other lifetime. But right now nothing is worse than the crushing shame and guilt connected to my time with the Sufi Order."

A few weeks later, I received a gracious short note from Pir Vilayat's secretary, telling me that he released me from any responsibilities to him or to the Order, and that he wished me well.

Not only did I never tell Alan about Pir Vilayat's pronouncement, I have told no one at all about it until this writing, forty-five years after the fact. Even now, I wake up suddenly in the night, thinking that, in revealing it, I have done something cosmically ruinous, something that on some plane of existence represents the most terrible betrayal. But as I get used to the idea of having released myself from this secret that mattered to no one but me, I know in my heart it's a liberation. Pir Vilayat often used to say, "Shatter your ideal on the rock of Truth," and here that dictum was finding serious application. Because there can hardly be a more powerful ideal than Enlightenment, I felt I had to defend that ideal with every ounce of my strength, at all costs keeping it safely removed from the rock of Truth. If I could preserve the possibility of my own enlightenment—sometime, somewhere—nothing else would matter.

I did not see that in doing so I was enshrining my interpretation of the Truth in place of the real thing. Definitely not a version of "Thy kingdom come, Thy will be done." More like a delicate blend of Golum and Miss Havisham. The Truth is a living thing, not subject to the mental taxidermy of anyone. When Pir Vilayat said to me, "If things go according to plan" what was the "plan"? It might be that I would not—in this lifetime, anyway— be a transformed consciousness. It might be that, in this lifetime, I should keep a stranglehold on his words, strap them to myself like a hair shirt for forty years, and learn something from the act of eventually letting go.

That would be enough.

Whatever it ends up looking like, at least it will be the Truth.

31.

After a year at Alan and Helen's, I was increasingly dogged by the question of when I should leave. I was nearly thirty, and living a life that had more in common with a fifteen-year-old. My parents called from time to time, asking discreet questions. My sister, too, was gently curious about my plans. Whenever I brought up the issue to Alan, he always gave me the same response: Don't worry, you'll know.

Tied up as I was in hellish knots, I could never have guessed the obvious answer. Though my discussions with Alan were potent and inspiring, they were, after all, verbal exercises, subject to the mind's control. The only force that would be strong enough to crack my will and ultimately get me out of Ojai was the wad of hormones that lies in wait, ready to overwhelm every young man in some fashion, sooner or later.

In late spring of 1979, with Ojai's skies brilliantly blue and its carpets of wildflowers still breathtaking, I was ambushed by this powerful explosive substance, detonating in my body. On a visit to a department store in Ventura, in search of a birthday present for my mother, I couldn't help but notice that the young woman behind the counter was attractive. With short brown hair, huge green eyes, and skin that seemed to glow, she was wholesome-looking and approachable enough to make the process of buying a scarf enjoyable.

It was not until I had driven all the way home that I woke up to the situation. That young woman was *beautiful*. And sweet. She didn't seem to mind my badgering her about various scarves. So why didn't I—I don't know—*ask her out*, or something? I could do that, couldn't I? Just because I was living at Alan and Helen's didn't mean I couldn't go on a date. I wasn't a monk. Still, it seemed ridiculous. Aside from the impossible relationship with Sister Ellen, I hadn't had anything that even vaguely qualified as a romantic thought for years. I tried to think of the last time I had made love. Sometime in 1974, five years before, with Jessie.

I could've kicked myself for not saying anything. I didn't even get her name. Back at the house, I went straight into my room and found the phone book. I called the store's general information number. Though it took some talking, Leslie eventually agreed to have dinner with me at the Ranch House. I was unnerved but jubilant.

The dinner was perfect. The beautiful night, the scallops in herbed *beurre blanc*, the Joseph Matrot Meursault-Charmes—everything converged to make me a guilty, anxious wreck. Only my iron determination not to embarrass myself saw me through. What was especially touching was the kindness of the crew. Dan Moynier showed up as our wine steward, and did a great job of being deadpan and deferent. I did get annoyed when one of the busboys stood behind Leslie's chair and gave me a big thumbs up. Just a hint of a scowl from me, though, and he was gone.

Her wonderful sleeveless linen dress fit so well I was embarrassed to look at her, figuring I must be gawking. It was terrible that I paid almost no attention to anything she said. I just looked and then looked some more. My chatter was absent-minded; just something to make sure she stayed in her chair and let me ogle her.

Driving her home, I was seized by anxieties about the goodnight scene at the front door. Here I was on this date I had worked so hard to arrange, and now I was aware just how little self-assurance I had. Looking casual was unimaginably hard work; I was in a cold sweat.

Luckily, someone was in control. Standing at the door she kept up a soothing patter, as if I were a skittish horse. She seemed to be standing unnaturally close. The porch light caught her hair, giving it a burnished, brilliant look. "Well," she said at length, "I had a great time. And you seem like a really nice guy." Her eyes seemed a mile deep, full of sympathy (for what?) and gentle encouragement. I lightly rested a hand on each of her shoulders, leaned over, and kissed her. I did not lose consciousness, but for a moment it seemed a high probability. When I leaned away from her, though my eyes were not focusing properly, I saw a big, warm smile on her face. "Now that wasn't so bad, was it?" she said softly.

We both chuckled nervously. I cradled her face in my hands and gave her a longer kiss. Longer, but still disgracefully chaste. I said goodnight and walked back to my car on rubbery legs.

The next morning at breakfast I told the whole story to Alan. "He smiled and shook his head. "My, but that little thing" – he held up his index finger—"can get you into all kinds of situations you might not have bargained for. Are you going to see her again?"

I hesitated. "You know, I'm really not sure, Alan. I guess I might."

I never did.

But there was a new phenomenon that arose from my date with Leslie: erections. Since that morning in 1975 when I woke up in Hell, there had been none. No sexual feelings at all. I had run into all sorts of attractive women at the restaurant, around Ojai and elsewhere, but my sense of shame at being a fundamentally failed person kept me from being the slightest bit assertive with women, and eliminated the urge to participate in the ritual of sending and receiving the cues that are part of dating/mating. The most I had been able to manage was to put out a silent wounded puppy-dog sympathy plea, which momentarily got the attention of the maternal set, but which the great majority of women treated as a virulent social leprosy. So it was a shock to wake up one morning, a few days after the date, with an unambiguous hard-on.

My first thought was: "I must be becoming a human being again." Lying in bed, I thought of how amazing it would be to go out and find a sexual partner. I could do that, after all, couldn't I? I could even get married, be a regular person! I was dizzy with possibilities.

With the hormonal floodgates open and my emotions

easily spilling out, I soon found myself in another relationship, longer but still chaste. It was hopeless from the start—she, working at the restaurant for the summer, nearly ten years my junior and a good Catholic on top of it—but discrimination was not part of my new-found, turbulent emotional life. Though she was beautiful and smart, her parents' disapproval and my own confusion finally tipped the scales.

I was bruised and frustrated, spending the summer lost in the hormone hurricane, irritable in an expertly passive-aggressive way. My headaches became more frequent, and I made them worse by speaking silently to them, welcoming them, daring them to do their worst. There were those erections too, showing up most often just as I awakened in the morning. I could hardly bear to be around people, so my work at the restaurant became excruciating.

One morning at breakfast I finally boiled over. As soon as I sat down, the look of frank concern on Alan's face told me he knew things had taken an especially bad turn.

I took a sip of tea and folded my arms in front of me. "Okay, so we might as well get started. Here I am, the C-plus student, ready to try answering one of your questions and ready to be told I don't quite have it right. Better luck next time and all that."

Alan's glance was gentle but very direct. "What do you mean?"

"Oh, come on Alan, you know very well what I mean. It's always the same. You ask me what the connection is between thought and emotion—or whatever—and I give you an answer, which I have barely

229

gotten out of my mouth before you say, 'Not so fast!' or 'Don't jump!' or 'Think!' or 'Don't think!' I mean, don't you get tired of having such a dull, slow-witted student around? Couldn't we find you a better one somewhere? Why should you have to put up with this?"

Helen spoke up. "I just don't think you're seeing this clearly, my dear. I don't think you're right."

I jumped on that. "And you're both very condescending to me most of the time, by the way. It's horrible being condescended to every day of your life, I'll tell you."

Alan was silent. He kept his eyes on me, expressionless, except for what looked like a very faint smile at the corners of his mouth.

"That's silly. I'm not condescending toward you at all." said Helen, matter-of-factly.

"Are you kidding? You're being condescending to me *right now*, Helen." I was barking at her.

After a moment, Alan spoke. "I don't think I ever told you about my row with my teacher, Jenny Bollenbacher, a couple of years before she died?"

"No, I don't believe you ever did."

"Well, as I told you, I did everything she asked of me for many years. But there came a time when I had my own ideas about how to do things at the Theosophical lodge. Oh lord. She told me in no uncertain terms that I was to follow her instructions, period. I blew up at her for the first time. I said, 'You're not my teacher!', and she shot back, 'You're not my student!'" He chuckled. "Luckily, we made it up before she died."

"So, you think that's what we're doing here?" I asked.

"I am not brave enough to say that definitively, no. Please take it in the helpful spirit in which it was offered."

"Fair enough. And I hope you'll take my suggestion in the same way. Wouldn't this be easier with a B-plus student? Or maybe there isn't any such thing. We might just be living in a world crawling with C-plus people. That's more like how it looks to me."

Alan looked at me with frank affection. "My dear friend, exploration is rarely easy. It can be extraordinarily difficult, as we have both discovered at various moments." He paused. "I'll bet this sounds condescending to you, does it?" He sipped his coffee.

"As a matter of fact, yes, it does."

"I understand. Why don't we skip the discussion today? There is a lot to do at the restaurant, anyway. I promised to go over to Ventura and get some more flats of pansies for those beds under the trees. Would you be willing to come along and help me?"

And of course I did. But I was simmering inside for days, with all the same, monotonous, teeth-gritting questions. How did I get shipwrecked like this? Who was responsible? I wanted names. I was an American Catholic kid who didn't seem any crazier or more foolish than any of my peers, but who ended up lost in a psycho-spiritual spookhouse from having overdosed on a perfectly legal substance: asceticism. I couldn't seem to get myself "normal" again, but I couldn't seem to be able to go completely insane, either. As if there were just enough Little League Baseball and Saturday morning cartoons in my battered, exhausted memory to allow me to take a wine order at the restaurant, but not enough to allow me to ditch all the religious phantoms and just be a guy, maybe a husband and father, maybe a Rotary member. The beauty and power of the ecstatic state? It's hard to admit, but for a while I seriously thought that feigning indifference might be a good strategy for regaining it. Being at Alan and Helen's might be all wrong. Too obvious, too desperate. Like trying to attract a desirable person: put on a show and make sure they see you, but don't follow them around like a dog. I was applying high school dating techniques to my attempts at regaining meditative states. An interesting gambit, but doomed to failure because of, among other things, what I came to call the Truth of the Reliquary.

Reliquaries, you might recall, are the containers, large and small, usually made of precious metals, jewels, and glass, that house various physical remains of Catholic saints. A small, jewel-encrusted tube for the ring finger of Theresa of Avila, a miniature gold chapel for the femur of Anthony of Padua. Whatever. On first seeing examples of these, it is easy to be horrified and label them barbaric and ghoulish—and on one level that is certainly true. But on the other side of the coin, it is clear that the actual presence of the saints made such an impression on people that, after their deaths, people decided they would much rather have a moldy finger than nothing at all. And this is the definition of my predicament: I could not forget those extraordinary meditative states—though the memory now might be putrid and boring to myself and others—because they were so real, so overwhelmingly powerful. Who am I kidding? I am programmed to keep the moldy finger. It's all I've got.

After a few days of planting flowers at the restaurant, weeding the beds, fixing the little fountain in the back yard at the house, Alan and I seemed ready to have discussions again. On the way back from another visit to the nursery, we did a kind of post-mortem on my outburst. Alan said, "I think it was necessary, lad. And I honor it." I looked at this man who was driving his big white Cadillac, and I saw again how much he and Helen had done for me—and for so many others. I was some aging waif who had shown up on their doorstep, and they opened their lives to me completely.

"Alan, how can I ever repay you for everything you've done for me?" I said, with a catch in my voice.

He kept his eyes on the road as he said, "Do the same for another, my friend. Do the same for another."

32.

Enter Veronique. She was the goddess I would have had to invent had she not existed. She was a comet in the firmament, awe-inspiring and ominous. Her brilliant, fiery presence was enough to pull me out of Ojai permanently (the unambiguous force Alan had predicted) and to convince me that, at last, I had encountered the person who would shatter my ruinous obsession with the memory of heaven. She would bring me back to life.

She came to the restaurant with three friends on a cold, clear night in March of 1980. I waited on the table and was immediately smitten. She had the gamine, tomboy appearance I always favored, more striking than conventionally beautiful. Large hazel eyes set a bit too far apart, sensuously proportioned mouth, silky blonde pageboy falling to her strong jaw line. I couldn't help but notice the way her cashmere sweater draped gracefully on her small frame.

And she was French. With her full-throated contralto, in gorgeously, theatrically-accented English, she identified herself as the daughter of a prominent wine producer in Burgundy's Cote de Nuits. I was defense-less. We spoke mostly in French—about wines we ad-mired, about her family, about Ojai. She told me I should come up to Berkeley the following Wednesday for a tasting of new imports being handled by the wholesaler she worked for. I laughed.

The next morning, Alan was sitting at his place sip-ping tea when I sat down. Helen was not up yet.

"Alan, I think I'm in love." I looked at him, daring him to mock me.

His eyebrows shot up and he smiled gently. No trace of teasing. "Really! Tell me."

I recounted the story. "And the craziest part is, she invited me to this tasting—a trade tasting at her compa-ny's offices—next Wednesday. I mean, give me a break. I had to explain to her that in Ojai we don't tend to move that fast. I told her maybe they do in San Francisco, but not here."

Alan looked nonchalant. "You're going, aren't you?"

I was incredulous, then flustered. "Well…yes. Yes, I suppose I am."

I showed up at the tasting only to find Veronique standing in the middle of the room, surrounded by a swarm of men. As I so often did over the next month, I fought crushing self-doubt. What did I expect? Men must be taking a number to get a date with this attrac-tive, cosmopolitan French woman. So she happened to travel to the barely-civilized outpost of Ojai, where she ran into a sommelier at a local restaurant. So what? What would have led me to believe I could hold this woman's attention for longer than fifteen minutes?

Staying each time with my sister who now lived in San Francisco, I made four short forays into Veronique's world, battling for her attention with the determination of someone convinced of his destiny. I was decisive, assertive, world-wise—all completely out of character.

After the third visit, when I had seen real interest and affection in Veronique's eyes, I was slapped around by my gravest doubts. Why did this woman seem to like me? Okay, I'm not disgusting looking; and I can even be charming sometimes. For very short stretches. But how will she feel about an intimate relationship with someone who has spent years being damned? What happens when she discovers that it's taken me years even to begin crawling out of the twisted wreckage of hardly bearable experiences, that I'm living in an undeclared halfway house in Ojai, receiving daily counseling? And, at thirty years of age, that I can hardly find my way to the figurative men's room? And sex, what about sex? Just the thought of it with Veronique plunged me into the most anxious, humiliating, wonderful imaginings. I would be helpless to do anything that seriously resembled performance, that was certain. Should I avoid the whole relationship now, before it was too late?

Hah.

Back in Ojai, I had a dream one night. I was lying in my bed, in my little room at Alan and Helen's, when an angel appeared. A serene, effulgent light surrounded the androgynous creature, with its long blond hair and flowing white robe. I got out of bed and knelt down on the carpet. I said, "I am so thankful for this visit, it is such comfort! What words do you have for those of us who are struggling to find our way through the thicket of human life? What can you say to us, we who go from day to day, feeling lost in the fog of this existence? What message have you brought to console the souls here below, who have no desire except the one desire for Truth?"

The angel looked at me with unbearable sweetness. Offering the barest hint of a guileless smile, in a voice that had the clarity of some fantastic reed instrument, it said, "Shut up and live."

That became a new mantra for me as I suffered through the days between my now routine trips north. It was hard to focus on work; it was even hard to concentrate on the morning discussions with Alan. He was patient, as usual. "You mustn't underestimate the power of this feeling," he said one morning. "If it was enough to launch a thousand ships, it is more than worth observing." He laughed softly. "Though I imagine observation is not your first response. But of course all of this is happening now because you are ready for it."

On my fourth trip north, Veronique and I spent the night together for the first time. The lead-up to the event was anything but promising. As we sat in a restaurant sipping the last of our wine, she announced that she had always had unwanted psychic visions. As a child, walking through rows of her family's vineyards in the early morning, she had encountered men and women wearing strange, crude clothing, speaking in a barely-recognizable ancient French dialect. They were gone as quickly as they appeared. Looking at the faces of people she encountered in her daily life, she would sometimes see visions of their future and past. The experiences upset and frightened her; she had tried to ignore them but found she could not.

. I didn't show my exasperation, but asked myself testily why this psychic stuff— part of Alan's story as well—seemed to be following me around. I never really trusted it. After a silence, she gave me a serious look and said, "I must tell you something. It will seem strange to you." She paused, waiting for me to acknowledge this.

I said "Fire away." What I thought was: This can't be good.

"I am jealous of your past."

"Pardon me?"

She pursed her lips, looking impatient. "I knew this would not be easy, but you must hear me out. I can see that you are very old. I have always had this way of looking at people that tells me things about them. About their pasts, a long time back. In your case, I have seen you several times with the *capuchin*...how do you say that in English?"

"That means 'cowl,' I think. The hood that is part of a monk's robe?"

"Exactly. You have been a monk many times. Sometimes—forgive me—you were powerful, but not always strong." She saw that I was having a hard time with what she was saying, especially with my head full of wine.

"I see the doubt in your eyes, but I must say you are wrong to doubt. Simply because you do not have the experiences does not mean it is wise to dismiss this truth, even if it is a little...expanded. Beyond what you know."

She invited me to her apartment, a large, perfectly

renovated 40s-era flat. It was beautiful, she was beautiful; I was more convinced than ever that the relationship was fated.

Not more than a few steps inside the door, she turned to face me. We clasped hands and just looked, for a moment. We leaned toward each other slowly and kissed. She didn't close her eyes, nor did I mine. Then she did a strange thing. She giggled delightedly, putting an open palm on one side of my face and the tip of her right baby finger into my mouth. I could hear my own breath.

Without another word, we moved to the bedroom and shed our clothes. I was in a panic. I had to say something to her. "Veronique. I have not been with a woman in more than five years."

She laughed. "You are such a liar!"

I tried to tell her the story without really telling her. After all, here we were, lying naked on her bed—what would be the point of getting into a *long, dreary story now*? But I knew I would have to explain my inability to perform, and I thought, why not get ahead of the curve? I talked about being alone for long periods, about fasting and meditation. I talked about some of the bits of Buddhism in the purple book. This was not a great strategy. Not terrifically sexy. Finally, after a silence, I touched her hair and said, "It takes my breath, Veronique. Being here takes my breath."

She smiled sweetly and said, "Not quite all of it, I notice."

When we were both satisfied that the main event would have to be postponed indefinitely, Veronique said, "When you are home, you will think of this many times."

"You're telling me."

The following Friday night, there was sex. No food, no wine, no music, and just about as little foreplay as there was conversation. I wish I could say it was some revelatory experience for me (or for her), some dramatic turnabout in the mindset of a person who had been damned and lost. Instead, it was like a carnival ride. A rush of exhilaration that leaves you dizzy, disoriented, a little nauseous. I had forgotten what sex was, or rather, how it felt. As great as it was, it was depressing, too, because while I was stunned by the beauty of it, I realized that my revelations of 1974 were correct: the feelings that flooded me during the times of Joy and Ecstasy were far beyond anything that sex had to offer. Even sex with Veronique. It wasn't even an interesting contest.

I was not crazy enough to talk with her about any of this. I held it inside, just another sadness.

33.

One overcast morning, I was in the kitchen after breakfast, doing the dishes. I could hear the shower going in Helen's bathroom, and I thought Alan had gone to his room to get dressed. I heard shuffling behind me and felt a hand on my shoulder. It was Alan, still in his robe, looking at me with that hooded-eye glance of his, focused but gentle. "My dear friend," he said quietly, "you have to accept your fate before you can find out what it is." He turned and walked back to the hallway that led to his room.

A gust of wind blew through me. I was seized by a sudden urge to race after him and ask exactly what he meant, ask him if we could talk about it. Just as quickly, that feeling passed—mostly because on some level I knew *exactly* what he meant. I couldn't chase after him to have him tell me what to do. What was needed was some looking, and Alan couldn't do it for me. Ever. It was to be a full-time job, then. The Magnum Opus. A life's work. The pale morning light glowed on the tile countertop as I began again, rinsing dishes, putting them into the dishwasher.

When I finally announced that I would be moving in with Veronique, it was an acknowledgement of the obvious. Alan and Helen were jubilant, but a bit wistful, too. I felt a surge of powerful affection for these two people who had recognized my horrendous malaise and had had the generosity to scoop me up and reintroduced me to life when I felt my sheer toxicity would keep anyone from ever befriending me. It was—and I don't say it lightly—a miracle. In the years following my departure, Alan wrote me a number of letters, many of which were signed "with much love (though I know you don't like the word)." He was right, I didn't like the word. Though I still prefer that it be used sparingly, and insist that whatever it represents remain a mystery, the greatest of mysteries, in expressing my feelings toward Alan and Helen I use it wholeheartedly.

In the weeks before I moved north, Veronique and I met for a few days here and there, in various locations—Carmel, Big Sur—but we seemed to relish most the time at her place in Berkeley. We bought cheeses and *charcuterie* and produce at the little specialty shops on Shattuck Avenue. We took turns cooking dinner for each other.

Little by little, I told her details about my obsessive life. She showed little interest in the purple book or in Krishnamurti's works. Sufism was least interesting of all to her. It was strange that nothing I told her seemed to shock her. Through the lens of her simmering, psychic, Gallic self, it all seemed almost normal, and to be expected. I thought: This woman eats crazy for breakfast!

I threw everything I had at her, and she was unfazed. This experiment could work.

But even in recounting the story to her, I could feel the remains of my willfulness, wedged as it was between its rock and its hard place. When in my mind I heard Alan saying, "You can't know God," there was a voice in me still wanting to say, "Fuck that! I say I can!" But I knew from experience that a blindly stubborn direct assault on reality was a poor strategy. I knew, too, that someone with my mindset could not approach the states I had been in six years before. Anyway, I would have been afraid even to try. I was sure the effort would kill me.

So now I was going to get there some other way. Say, just for example, through a relationship with a fierce, psychic Frenchwoman. I knew I needed to give up control once and for all, to break down even further the tunnel-vision dedication of the "little man" Alan had seen sitting inside me, so resolute, so blind, so much a Catholic kamikaze. Being with Veronique seemed as good a way as any to do just that, to stop being so wound up about Holiness (whatever that is) and just enjoy being with another person. Enjoy some good wine and some sex. Learn to be a human being, a regular guy.

There was a hitch, of course. To be a regular guy, I knew I needed to display for Veronique a range of solid male responses to the world. Competent Male Protector responses that indicated focus and direction, the determination to pee on some territory, feather a nest, make a mark in the world that she and others would recognize. I desperately wanted to parade in front of her with a peacock tail, but vaguely understood that not only was

I not going to be capable of it at that moment, but that I would *never* be. I couldn't quite see that this was a matter of my not being suited to the kind of life I thought I wanted. In my view, it was still a sign of basic deficiency, yes, but even more, a punishment for having the hubris to imagine I could explore the darkest caverns of myself and return with a gold nugget. That I could reach God.

These realizations came to me only after moving into Veronique's apartment and getting a job as wine buyer for a shop in San Francisco, the former turning out to be only slightly less a uniform misery than the latter. It was only my sheer stubbornness, my sense of the inevitability of the relationship, that kept me going. This was clearly not enough for Veronique.

One evening, when I had tossed a quote from the purple book into our conversation, as I often did, Veronique got testy. "Don't you get tired of your search for Authority? Okay, so you don't have a good relationship with your father, understood, but this constant mooning after teachers is absurd! Your Sufis, your Buddhas, enough is enough, don't you think?"

I had been poked and prodded by her like this before, but for whatever reason this time it was especially irritating. "Is all of this by way of telling me how much you like my company? Lots of analysis and criticism? Because if it is, I'd rather go down to the café on Birchwood and leave you in peace for a while."

She raised her voice. "Oh yes! This is your way of dealing with things—by *not* dealing with them! Go ahead, walk away! You love destroying everything so much, even yourself!"

"That is *ridiculous*."

She looked at me sidelong for a moment, with real disdain. "I have not told you anything of what I saw last week. But this might be as good a time as any."

"What do you mean by that?"

"I mean I had images of you in the past."

"So we're back to the monk again?"

She looked even more peeved. She crossed her legs. "More than that. I was feeling angry with you when the images came to me, so I did not pay much attention and did not see many details. You were living in France, many centuries ago, in a well-off family, but your father thought little of you. He ignored you most of the time, though you constantly looked for his approval. You felt guilty about not living up to his expectations. You became a monk to please him. It did nothing. You learned the skills of a warrior too, and still he ignored you. Finally, there was a war, and you distinguished yourself by taking many foolish risks. You would get far out ahead of your horsemen in charging the enemy. What did you want? You wanted to be killed in battle, to prove your worth to your father." She stopped for a moment, looking satisfied to have shocked me. But her expression lost focus; she looked aside, like she had heard a noise in the distance. Then she continued, more slowly. "No. No, that wasn't what you wanted at all. What you really desired was to be taken prisoner by your enemies, and…and tortured to death." She blinked a few times, then looked at me and continued. "In the end, you were mortally wounded on the battlefield, and as you died you realized that it would change nothing about how your father saw you. Your guilt and inadequacy were still there."

I looked coolly at her. "I'm sorry to see you use your special talents to score debating points."

"I am telling you only what I saw. If it is not useful to you, you should discard it."

"I am not going to fight with you, Veronique, though you might really want me to."

She paused, looking at me grimly. "What are we doing together, really?"

It was the question that shattered my ideal. I had enough pride to walk out the door the next morning, buy a newspaper, look at the rental ads, and find a place of my own. Once settled in that tiny studio apartment, I could finally acknowledge the illusion of seeing myself together with Veronique. And I could make a juicy meal out of the loss, the rejection. But then, naturally, almost as an afterthought: Could this failure and the suffering it brings be a path back to the state of Joy and Beauty? That bit was especially maddening.

34.

PAX VOBISCUM

The first mail I received at my new address was a letter from Alan. It was a mild and sunny day in late fall, so I took a chair out onto my little balcony that overlooked part of the UC Berkeley campus, and sat down to read:

My Dear Friend,

I hope you are well in the midst of all the turmoil. Surely none of the pain you are experiencing now seems useful or beneficial. The rawest pain never does. It rather invites our mind to explain it, hoping to make it a little more bearable. But though that response is built into us, any kind of interpretation, "making sense" of events, can only be an attempt to avoid being fully present with what is actually happening now. And that is why I am writing to you.

I read an article about Evolution in the L.A. Times the other day, describing fresh evidence gathered in Ethiopia, about our predecessors in time. It compared the nearly-human remains found there to those found at other sites in Africa, in China, and elsewhere, speculating about the chronologies, physical differences, and their relationship to homo sapiens. It was fascinating. And then just last night I was awake in the dark of the very early hours (as you know I so often am) and I saw something I wanted to tell you about.

It is this: You are right on time. There is no need to fuss about it, no need to hurry, but— pick up the golden thread and walk on. Maybe this is what Evolution is about, this procession toward something unknown; not just the flowering of larger brains in larger skulls, but experiences such as the ones you had. Ecstasy may yet be our birthright—that, and whatever is beyond it. Ultimately, your experiences will not alienate you from others, because as part of Evolution they are about our future life as a species, as a planet, as a cosmos, the vast unstoppable thing we have no name for—is it God? Love? Whatever you call it, it will overcome every attempt to be small and safe and crafty and separate. Because it is *our* voyage together, one that never ends, full and complete as it moves through time.

With much love (though I know you don't like the word),

Alan

I read the letter again, then folded it and put it back in the envelope. I looked out over the rooftops and trees of the Berkeley hills. The ecstatic state as evolutionary phase—it had never occurred to me. Though much later I would discover it was hardly a new idea, at that moment I felt just how right Alan was, if only in the idea that as time passes human bodies and minds will reach for new and un-heard of capacities, as we did with, say, speech and writing. That urge, that drive, will certainly overcome conformity and the terrible social morality that always seems to enslave us. Though the world still dearly loves a cage, in the end we are all daring escape artists, willing or no.

Reliably, my brain kicks in, asking questions and more questions. It wants to know when and why and all the rest of it. Isn't it hopeless, it asks, if it's taken all this time to get us to a place in the West where a few million people are doing Power Yoga, or Aerobic Yoga, or Low Impact Step Yoga for Seniors? Alan's letter is sitting in its envelope in my lap, but it seems to be prompting me, as if we were still sitting around the table in Ojai some morning, saying the heart of it is that we absolutely *will* keep moving, and become more astonishing and fulfilled and that it is none of our business how it will happen or how long it will take. Those details are thankfully safe from all tampering, held in the silent reaches of some fathomless other dimension.

I felt sheepish then, thinking how ferociously, over a period of five years, I had clung to the hope of returning myself to Ecstasy (There was Alan again, saying "My God, you're willful!"). It was, after all, more the panic of the addict in search of a fix than the dedication of the devotee. How obvious could it be that my own extreme pleasurable sensations were never the issue, were never going to be the feature presentation? Yet I couldn't fault myself, either, since it was the blinding power of the experience that evoked an equally strong attachment. When you come upon something so extraordinary, so far beyond anything you have known before, it makes sense to say: "Right! I'm going to get a map to this spot, and come back with a bunch of Coleman coolers and a U-Haul trailer! I wonder if the stuff is patented?" Let's face it, if it were a more ordinary discovery, one would likely say, "Okay, that was great. But I've *got* to get going and make some guacamole. The NBA playoffs are on in half an hour!"

Though I am now rarely overcome by the sharp stab of nostalgia and the caught-at-the-throat feeling of unendurable loss, I can't pretend that the memory of Ecstasy—and what it represented—is not still with me. Will the search ever end? My guess is it won't. Not completely. Even now, if some archangelic master of ceremonies were to appear and propose a sure-fire method for regaining that state of being, would I do what was asked? Or does the rock of truth need to shatter not just all the methods of approach, but even the state of Ecstasy itself, this great ideal I have carried in my chest for so many years like a disease, like a burning coal? I can almost see Lucifer—that willful and proud creature, refusing to bend his knee—as the ultimate idealist. He knows how the universe could be improved. He'll explain it all to you. And you can be like a god with him, theorizing in some ovenly corner of the cosmos, carefully considering in the most dazzling abstraction all the ways in which our world is a failure. I spent a lot of time in that discussion group, and I can tell you: it's pretty hollow stuff. Trust me.

There is no tidy ending to a tale like this one. An obscure subject matter hitched to an idealist's maddening obsession, trailing too many loose ends. I don't insist now that I make a list of lessons learned, that it should spell out some recipe for perfection or the first chapter of the ultimate self-help book. I know better now than to mix up that volatile cocktail of ideals and will power.

The simple truth is that Life is bigger even than Ecstasy. So any trust, any allegiance, any faith that I have must go to the living, flowing, and unpredictable truth that lies in Being Here Now; and not in even the strongest memory, the most life-like emotional and spiritual taxidermy. Alan said it best when I first met him in Switzerland: I have enormous faith. Not in anything or anyone in particular. Just enormous faith.

35.

EPILOGUE — THE BIRD WITH THE SILK KERCHIEF

Within two years of parting ways with Veronique, with a small group of Englishmen I helped found a winery business that produced nearly 150,000 cases of California wine each year. Over time, though I could never completely shake the notion that all my experiences amounted to little more than the dutiful consumption of bowl after bowl of thin gruel, I experienced the satisfaction of knowing that something I made had provided people with enjoyment.

It was both a blessing and a curse to live with my obsessive nature during those years. I found out that much could be accomplished in a sixteen- or seventeen-hour work day, even though many of those days were spent working maniacally. Harder, not smarter. Often they were days that satisfied only my compulsion to push beyond physical and mental limits, much like I had done in my meditative quest for understanding. Also much like what my father had done when trying to finish a script late at night, drifting into exhausted unconsciousness, falling to the floor, then getting back up in his desk chair to try to continue working.

I joke with myself sometimes by reciting a little prayer I composed: Lord, give me the wisdom to accept those things that are hard-wired into the system.

I have returned to France many times in the years since 1980, and each time I am aware of the peculiar strong connection I feel with the country and its people. I never seem to tire of my visits, though when I tell friends where I am planning to vacation, their response is inevitably the same: "Why not try somewhere else for a change?" From time to time I have taken their advice, and almost always find myself saying, "This is interesting, but I could be in *France*!" There is no doubt that for me a visit to France is a form of nourishment that occurs on many levels, but I don't try too hard to dissect it.

Many friends from both countries insist that I am actually more French than American, though I have not a single drop of French blood in my known heredity.

I have not married—at least thus far—nor have I had children. These facts touch off nearly as much speculation among my friends as they do from time to time in my own mind. Veronique would certainly point to the influence of the *capuchin*. I don't discount that.

My continuing return to Life in the years following those recounted in this book has been very much like emerging from a coma. In films, we tend to see people coming out of comas abruptly, I suppose because it is more dramatically satisfying and condensed; but my understanding is that a gradual emergence from the comatose state is far more common, often over a period of months or even years. This is more like what I have known over the last forty-odd years: an almost imperceptible thinning of the clouds, a slight shift in the wind from time to time. A little perspective where before there was none.

I have had powerful help over the years from many of the people portrayed in this book, particularly, until his death in 1993, from my great friend Alan Hooker; and from Sister Ellen, who after 50 years continues her extraordinary work as a member of the Sisters of Mercy. Dan Moynier remained in my life like a mysterious comet, making intermittent, startling appearances until his death in 2007, at age 59.

Though I have not had contact with her in many years, Jessie married a wonderful man with a lot of heart, and as far as I know still lives in Ojai, where the family moved to allow their two children to attend a private school established by Krishnamurti.

Veronique married a French chef in the mid-eighties, and now divides her time between France and California.

The impression of life I am most often left with now, as the months and years go by, is one of immensity. My favorite image, the one that conveys this best, is an old story the roots of which I am uncertain. It is a description of how long it will take for all beings to realize their Buddhahood.

Imagine a solid block, a mountain of granite ten miles long, ten miles wide, and a mile high. Every one hundred years, a bird flies by with a silk kerchief in its beak, and brushes it against the block. The time it takes to wear down the block entirely is the time it will take for all of us to see What We Truly Are. What I love about this is: it describes something that is inevitable. As long as there are birds and silk kerchiefs enough, we will all get there.

AFTERWORD, 2016

When I began writing this story ten years ago, I had to accept that I did not have satisfying answers to the questions it would pose: questions about consciousness, mania, addiction, memory, and regret. This particular version of the writing process would inevitably be more about exorcism than about finding reader-friendly plot devices that would arrange the events recorded here into a tidy package. I suspected that the inspirational uplift that readers often expect from books on "spiritual" topics was in this case likely to be more of a downdraft. My most realistic goal could only be to detail what had happened as best I could, inching my way toward a less murky vision of this life.

Then, one night in the winter of 2016, things changed. Not wildly, not dramatically, but clearly. After lying in bed in the small hours of so many thousands of mornings, launching question marks into deep space without any hope of a response, I had been grateful for even the painfully slow recovery that the passage of time allowed me. The occasional deep breath, a temporary slacking of muscle tension, an unrestrained belly laugh. But on this particular night, there was a new question: Who was it who decided that the departure of Ecstasy was an irretrievable loss that left only ruins where there once had been a life?

I myself had done it, of course. It was my decision. I could say, well, it wasn't my fault, I was plunged into hellish pain and isolation by the departure of the powerful joy brought on by my meditation practices. I could say no one in his right mind would ever create such misery for himself; it was some agency beyond me that had thrust me into such complete desolation. But I suddenly knew that wasn't true. Here is what was true: The ecstatic feelings that had swept me up in an unbearably loving embrace were, on that winter morning in 1975, moving on. They were changing, shifting into something altogether different, and I was being invited to go along, to take the next step in the great exploration of consciousness. Perhaps the next thing would be quieter, more subtle, something of another order. But I would never know, because I fell back into the willfulness that Alan referred to so often in his conversations with me. I decided that if I were not to be permanently granted the powerful Ecstasy that I had known for those previous four or five months, then I would refuse everything else. I would clench myself in a tight ball of nerve, muscle, and resentment, and stay that way until I could regain what I had lost. In that way I caused myself decades of such misery as I would never have wished on anyone, ever. I willed that pain into being. I willed my own sorrow, my isolation, my own sense of despair, and worse than that: I willed myself into forty-plus years of an alternate life, one in which I would have to hide the mainspring of my being, the heart of my heart, fearing that anyone who saw it would see the misery I had created, would see what I was sure was nothing but shame, a failure, a ruin.

It never occurred to me that I was standing in my own way, blocking the light. Lost in memory and regret, I had made it impossible for the curtain to come up on the second act.

When I caught a glimpse of these things, I wanted to apologize. But to whom? To the universe? To all those who had to deal with this person over so many years, as he nursed his poorly-concealed, self-inflicted wound? All of that. Most difficult and necessary of all, though, was the need to apologize to myself, asking for forgiveness that only I could offer. I understand now that forgiveness is the key that will allow me to move along to that next thing, whatever it may be. The next act.

ACKNOWLEDGEMENTS

The burden of reading this work in its earliest, most ungainly form fell to just a few courageous souls. Among those who offered valuable commentary and suggestions, more than ten years ago, were my sister Kris; Joann Yates; and—especially—Mary Wheeling of New Leaf Editing.

In the latter phases, I received many helpful suggestions again from my sister, and also from my friends Sharon Dellamonica, Don Spirlock (affectionately known as "The Spiv"), and from Roger Hagan. The real heavy lifting, however, was done by my amazing editor Laurie Chittenden, who fearlessly carved her way through the chaos I handed her, asking insightful questions and providing vital cues that gave shape to the story. I owe her a great debt for her tremendous skill and instinct.

Thanks to both Sharon Dellamonica and my sister Kris for their help in sorting through Brad Norr's many fine cover design concepts.

The contribution which actually gave *Seeking* a

heartbeat, however, was that of my "savory" partner (she rejects the adjective "sweet"), Rebecca Scharding. I am very grateful for her presence in my life, and for the fact that we can share so richly in so many of the same madnesses.

ATTRIBUTIONS

Epigraph
After the Ecstasy, the Laundry: How the Heart Grows Wise on the Spiritual Path (copyright 2000, by Jack Kornfield) Bantam Books

Song lyric on p.13: from "White Wine in the Sun" by Tim Minchin, 2009. All rights reserved.

Quotes on pp. 36, 43, 44, 47, 49, 87-8, 93, 96, 114, 118, 137-8: *Be Here Now* by Ram Dass (copyright 1971, Lama Foundation/Crown Publishing Group.) All references to, and quotes from, the "purple book" in this work refer to *Be Here Now*.

Quote on p. 52-3: *Dark Night of the Soul* by St. John of the Cross, translated and with an introduction by E. Allison Peers (copyright 1959 Doubleday Image Books).

Quotes on pp. 57, 58, 60: *Flight of the Eagle* by Jiddu Krishnamurti (copyright 1971, Krishnamurti Foundation Trust Ltd.) Harper Colophon Books.

Quotes on pp. 77, 78: *Bhagavad Gita* (translated by Juan Mascaro, trans., copyright 1962) Penguin Books Ltd.

Quote on p.119: *The First and Last Freedom* by Jiddu Krishnamurti (copyright 1954, Krishnamurti Foundation Trust Ltd.) Harper Collins Publishers

Quote on p. 128-9: *Toward the One* (copyright 1974, The Sufi Order U.S.A.)

Quote on p. 148: *The Book: On the Taboo Against Knowing Who You Are* by Alan Watts (copyright 1966, Alan Watts) Collier Books edition, published by arrangement with Pantheon Books, a division of Random House, Inc.

NOTE: Two statements offered to me by Alan Hooker as quotes of Krishnamurti appear in the book as he gave them to me, though they are only paraphrases of statements found in the archives of Krishnamurti's works. These are: p. 144, "Action from a thought is always false." And p. 161, "You're all so busy trying to paint a picture of the life you want. Why not let life paint its picture on you?"

CPSIA information can be obtained
at www.ICGtesting.com
Printed in the USA
LVHW040214021219
639107LV00001B/56/P

9 780984 794164